13-79

Studying
and Learning

DOUBLEDAY PAPERS IN PSYCHOLOGY

Consulting Editor

Eugene L. Hartley

Professor of Psychology, The City College, New York

Additional papers will be forthcoming. Some will be discussions of other subjects within the field of psychology. Some will review the same topics from different points of view.

You may enter your subscription for the series now so that you will be sure to receive on approval each paper as soon as it is published. The papers will be priced at no more than $1.00. Address COLLEGE DEPARTMENT, Doubleday & Company, Inc., 575 Madison Avenue, New York 22, N.Y.

Doubleday Papers in Psychology

Studying and Learning

By MAX MEENES
Professor and Head
Department of Psychology
Howard University

DOUBLEDAY & COMPANY, INC.
Garden City, N.Y.
1954

LIBRARY OF CONGRESS CATALOG CARD NUMBER 54-10740
PRINTED IN THE UNITED STATES OF AMERICA
AT THE COUNTRY LIFE PRESS, GARDEN CITY, N.Y.

Preface

At almost no point in his life would it be inappropriate for a thinking person to pause and take stock of his activities to see if he is pursuing his goals in a reasonable and efficient manner. Certainly during a man's school career it is wise, from time to time, to assess the efficiency of work habits, for most of us develop our methods of studying and doing our school work in a rather haphazard fashion. Rarely do we assess the requirements objectively, review the ways of attaining our objectives, or deliberately select and develop the particular methods most suitable under the circumstances.

In *Studying and Learning*, Professor Max Meenes offers you the basis for overhauling your study methods with an eye to improving adjustments to school requirements. Here is a Why, What, and How to study—but not in the customary form. It is a how-to-do-it paper, but not of the cookbook variety. This presentation approaches the problem of confronting school requirements by examining the alternatives in the context of the scientific principles of learning. You are not told simply, "This is the best way," you are introduced to the findings of research workers in their studies of learning, as they may be applied to problems of studying. Thus you are put in a position to decide whether you wish to follow "best procedures" or to assume the calculated risks of less efficient methods.

In addition to contributing to the solution of study problems, Professor Meenes provides an introduction to the study of human psychology. Starting here with a vital student concern, *how to study*, principles of human behavior are introduced in the applied context. The reader is led to a sound understanding of many principles of psychology as well as techniques of study.

Studying and Learning is written in a style that is readily understood. It reflects in its author the synthesis of teacher, research worker, and guidance counsellor. It is marred neither by moralizing nor by the advocating of tricks to get good grades. Instead it is a straightforward review of the problems that confront the student in his efforts to master college-level material and a simplified presentation of the results of many studies that are relevant. Professor Meenes takes cognizance of the different purposes and abilities of students and the variation in the problems posed by different subject-matters. In doing so he has made available a statement that should be helpful to all college students.

EUGENE L. HARTLEY
Consulting Editor
Doubleday Publications in Psychology

Contents

||||||||||||||||||||||||||||||||||||||||||||||||||||||||||||||||||||||||||||||||||||||||||||||||||||||||||||||||||||||||||||||||||||||||||||||||||||||||||||||||||||

Introduction

What Is Learning?

No one can teach you, but you may learn. Your teacher can direct your learning, can show you how materials are derived or related, and stimulate you to study. Whether or not you learn and what you learn depend upon what you yourself do, for learning is activity. It is a form of activity that may itself be learned and you can, therefore, learn how to learn and how to improve your learning. With an understanding of the psychology of the learning process, you will see why one form of motivation yields different results from another and why one method of study is superior to another.

Learning is acquiring new information, new or changed ways of responding, new understanding. The fundamental principles of learning are few and are not difficult to grasp. Learning, like any other activity, must be initiated and sustained by some driving force or motive. It is purposive—directed toward specific aims or goals. There must be some means of seeing what leads to the goal and what does not: a way of knowing what is right and what is wrong. When errors occur, they must be recognized as errors so that other responses can be substituted. This requires some form of appreciation of what is "right." Whatever is learned is mastered to some degree and the amount of mastery can be increased with additional practice of an appropriate kind. What is learned may be retained for later use. What has been learned can also help in future learning.

All of this can be seen in the case of a rat learning a maze. The animal is instigated to run by the hunger drive. The path he will gradually learn to traverse is determined by the need to reach the food in the goal box at the end of the maze in the fastest time possible. As he runs the maze, he comes to know which paths lead to the goal and which ones end in blind alleys. Every time he runs the maze he makes fewer errors and the correct way is reinforced or strengthened. Thus there is a gradual mastery of the path that leads to the goal. This route will then be forgotten unless it is reviewed or reinforced by additional trials from time to time. Having mastered this maze, the rat will be able to learn the next one in less time.

What Is Study?

An understanding of the process of learning can help to improve your studying because studying is a form of learning and obeys the same laws. Studying is that form of learning which is deliberately undertaken for the purpose of improving a skill, obtaining information, and acquiring understanding. It is the general name for all methods used to obtain mastery of school subjects. You may learn where your mother keeps the cookies, but if you want to learn about cookies or how to bake them, you will get better results if you study than if you rely upon casual experience.

Being a passive spectator at a football game will not teach you much about the sport. Closer, more attentive observation will enable you to see some order in what is taking place on the field and you will get a better conception of the game. Reading about the sport will add to your knowledge, and study will help you to understand and retain what you have read. Participation in practice would be the most effective kind of learning, and taking part in a game is the best test of the effectiveness of what you have learned. An analysis of what you did and failed to do in the game will help you to improve before the next game. The mastery of school subjects likewise cannot be attained by being a passive spectator in class. It requires close attention, study, participation in class discussion, taking examinations, and learning from practice and from analysis of test results.

Study is directed learning. You have learned your attitudes, habits, and values perhaps without deliberate choice. In studying, you set out to learn selected materials. But whatever you learn intentionally or accidentally may become a part of you, provided you make frequent use of your knowledge. If you study only to give material back to the teacher, it does not become a permanent possession. What you learn to keep adds to your growth and gives you power over some aspect of living. This kind of growth need not stop with maturity nor with the end of your school days.

Acquiring a Vocabulary

Different ways of studying produce different learning results. If you learn "by heart," you will not acquire much meaning. Studying for a special temporary purpose will result in learning restricted largely to meeting that momentary end. If you seek understanding and permanent possession, you will come closer to attaining your objective if you use a method appropriate to your aim.

Suppose you wanted to improve your vocabulary. Would you study the dictionary and memorize a few words every day? Perhaps you would begin at the beginning of the dictionary and choose all the words that are unfamiliar. You would never finish your task and you would soon be forgetting words almost as fast as you learned new ones. If you learned the words by heart and without understanding, you would use them inappriately. Solving word games or crossword puzzles would not improve your working vocabulary. Your selection of words would be determined by the puzzle maker and not by your own needs. You might learn that "anet" is a four-letter word that means "dill," but that word would be forgotten as soon as the puzzle is solved: it might be retained if you anticipated that it would come up again in next week's puzzle. The most you could learn in this way would be the kind of words used in crossword puzzles. You would not acquire a vocabulary useful for ordinary speech and writing.

How can you best acquire a useful vocabulary? Through extensive reading. The dictionary will be consulted for unfamiliar words so that your reading will be made more meaningful. You could do more: you could write each strange word on a card. Enter on the card not only the meaning of the word, but several phrases or sentences that show how the word may be used. These cards could be studied and reviewed at odd moments. If you also took every available opportunity to use these words in your speech and writing, you would add effectively to your vocabulary. As your vocabulary improves, your reading speed and comprehension will increase and your speech and writing will be more effective. You would thus gradually acquire an English vocabulary of increasing scope, one that would make your reading faster and more comprehensible.

Using cards in the same manner, you can best learn a foreign language vocabulary and the technical terms required for the understanding of each school subject. Every subject has its own distinctive vocabulary of technical words and symbols which will recur again and again. As these terms become more familiar through your study, they will be more quickly recognized. When you know them well, you will comprehend your technical material more rapidly.

Learning How to Study

In an experiment on problem-solving, it was found that monkeys improved their problem-solving ability by practice. They learned how to learn. Your own study also may be made more effective by your understanding of learning principles. Any new method of study, however, is at first used unskilfully. A new study method must be learned, and the student will find that his proficiency in its use will increase as he continues to practice with the better techniques.

Studying by wholes is often more efficient than studying by parts. It has been demonstrated by experiment that studying by the whole method gains in efficiency with increased practice over the more familiar study of the material one part at a time. Perhaps you have always memorized poetry by studying one line at a time. Should you now try to study by the superior method of reading the poem repeatedly from beginning to end, you may at first be disappointed in your results. The second time you try the whole method, you will improve because you will have acquired more skill in its use. With each attempt to use the new method you will progress until you have reached maximal efficiency. Every change in your method of study will have to be learned by practice with it.

It is hard to learn a new way of doing something; it is even more difficult to learn a new method when an old established procedure has been accepted as satisfactory. When an infant is weaned from the bottle, he finds it hard to give up his earlier mode of feeding, and when he first attempts to eat from a cup his handling of the cup is inept. Unless you are convinced that your old habits of study are inadequate to your present need, it is unlikely that you will attempt to improve them; and only if you persist in using the improved method will you acquire sufficient skill to benefit from its use.

In this paper you will see how your study may be improved by bringing your methods into closer harmony with the principles of learning. Your present study procedures may appear satisfactory to you even though they could be improved. As you advance in school, you will be confronted with the need to learn more complex and larger amounts of material. You will fall farther and farther behind if you do not improve your study methods. The kind of study that got you by in high school may not be good enough for college. You may attempt to compensate by increasing your study time, but poor study methods are time wasters.

In addition to requiring more study because of longer assignments, college work demands a different quality of learning. Reliance upon mere memorizing will no longer suffice. There will be too much to memorize and you will have too little understanding of the material to satisfy your teacher. Slow reading may be good enough when your assignments are short, but in college you will have so much to read that an increased rate of reading will be a most welcome time saver. You will do well to examine your present methods of study in the light of the principles of learning and study as developed in this paper and set about at once to change your methods where improvement is indicated.

Do not wait until your present methods prove inadequate. It takes time and practice to acquire skill in the use of a new study technique. As in all new learning, the learner must be willing to take a risk. You must give up the old and venture upon something that you have not tried before. You must expect to be clumsy and inefficient in your first attempts with the new method, but you should persist in the faith that improvement will come with practice.

Summary

Learning is a change in behavior directed by needs and rewards. The behavioral change may be carried out more skilfully and retained more firmly with practice. The method of practice and the character of the motivation influence the efficiency of the learning. Studying is intentional learning undertaken most commonly for the purpose of mastering school subjects. It is governed by the principles of the learning process. An understanding of these principles will indicate how study may be improved in effectiveness. A change in study procedure must itself be learned, and skill in its use will improve with practice.

There are many ways to study and each one produces a different outcome at a different cost of time and effort. An example of some different ways of studying to obtain an enlarged vocabulary illustrates the effect of choice of method. A more extensive examination of methods of study will be the concern of this paper, the remainder of which will deal with the why, what, and how of study.

Having come thus far in your reading, why not test yourself to see what you have learned. Try, without referring to the preceding pages, to answer questions about this introductory section. What is learning? What are the fundamental principles of the learning process? What is study? How can you best acquire a technical vocabulary? Now add some questions of your own and answer them. At this point compare your answers with what you have just read in the pamphlet. Are you satisfied? If not, will you go on from here or take the time to reread section one, keeping these questions in mind so that they will serve to direct your rereading? If you do reread, try answering these questions again. Have you done better this time?

Study Motivation

Study Is Motivated

You may study for the fun of it. You are likely to study because you are convinced that it is rewarding. Study is the dependable way of learning school subjects. It enables you to pass your tests and meet the standards of accomplishment set by your teacher. It leads to a diploma and to a life career. Study produces learning. It is these rewards that motivate study.

The motivation for study is complex. You study to pass a test, to avoid failure, to remain in school, to make your parents proud, and to achieve vocational and personal aims. You may concentrate your study efforts on passing tests or on qualifying for a profession. These and many other motives combine to induce study. The kind of studying you do will depend upon the nature of your purpose. The amount of study will be determined by the strength of your purposes and the standard of achievement you set for yourself.

The motivation for study fluctuates in strength, usually rising with the approach of examinations and diminishing between tests. When the study drive is low, study may be neglected while the student follows other pursuits. The motivation for study may best be maintained at a high level if study is treated as a job with regular hours. Since it is desirable to study regularly a study schedule should be followed.

Study Is Purposive

Learning is the goal of study. You study in order to learn what interests you, what you believe useful to your later life career, what you anticipate will help you to do well on examinations. You will probably study differently to achieve these different purposes.

What are your study purposes? What do you want to learn? This will differ with the subject but it is likely that you will want a good grade in every course. You will therefore study in order to pass examinations. If this is your only aim you may achieve it, but you will find that you forget most of what you have learned once it has served its purpose. Such learning is likely to be temporary rather than lasting. If you wish to retain your learning for future use, your purpose will need to be a broader one than merely passing the course.

Later learning may be based on earlier learning. Especially in language and mathematics will you need to retain your earlier learning in order to advance. A second course in any subject is likely to require some knowledge of the first course. If you have not retained what you have learned you will need to relearn for more advanced study. You would therefore get ahead faster if your study purpose went beyond the passing of a course. The medical student knows that he cannot afford to forget after his examinations are over; he expects to continue studying all his life and he is aware that his later study must be built on what he learned earlier.

You want to learn what appears useful. Every school subject has potential usefulness. In some instances the value is obvious, as that of physiology for the medical student. Other subjects have cultural rather than occupational values. The same subject can have a vocational use for one student, a cultural value for another. Students come to the same class with different purposes. In a foreign language course some study merely to meet a requirement, others to acquire a reading knowledge, some because they anticipate travel. The same subject has different values for these students. The value you find in your course will be related to your learning purpose. The way in which you intend to use your learning is your study purpose.

Study is purposive since it aims at learning which can be put to use. How strong is your study purpose? The amount of time you spend in study in relation to the time given to other activities may be taken as a rough index of the strength of your study drive. When you find yourself doing something else rather than studying, your study motivation is low. It was generally observed that ex-GIs in college after World War II were more serious and so did better work than other students. They had a strong study drive. The nature of your study purposes and the strength of your drive will determine how much you will study.

Study is an activity that has as its purpose the mastery of school subjects. This is rewarded by grades, diplomas, vocational success, status, and approval from others. It can bring to the student the satisfaction of learning. The anticipation of such rewards induces the student to undertake and carry out study activities. Study does not occur of itself. It must be motivated. It is a learned activity that is instigated and sustained by the complexity of the student's purposes. Some of the drive that makes for study comes from the student's need to pass tests combined with his conviction that study is the road to his goal. Other motives that make for study are the student's pride in his school achievement and his educational goals. These drives to study are in response to outside needs. Study can also be self-motivating. Interest in the method and the effects of study on the acquisition of learning may become drives to study. This form of motivation, intrinsic in the study process, is itself the result of learning. It comes out of practice with study and a demonstration of the relation between study and learning. Thus study can be activated by a multiplicity of aims and by the learning process itself.

Study Is Necessary for Dependable Learning

While some learning may be picked up incidentally, the assured way to learn school subjects is by studying. Study is learning with intent to master a subject. In the absence of this intent, mastery cannot be depended upon and the little learning that may occur will be vague and inaccurate. It has been shown by psychologists that merely looking at material without intent to learn will not produce learning. You can look at the wallpaper of your room thousands of times without learning enough about the pattern to describe it. Another example of this is the learning of the telephone dial. Although you have looked at the dial hundreds of times while telephoning you have probably failed to learn the dial because you did not deliberately try to do so. Besides there is no need. It is always there when you want it, so why try to learn it? Possibly you believe that you have learned it without trying, since you have seen it so many times. Test yourself. Before reading any farther, draw a diagram of the telephone dial. Have you arranged all the letters and numbers just where they belong? Are the letters black or red? Where did you place the letter Q? Now compare your diagram with the actual dial. How close did you come? Were you surprised because you made some errors although you felt certain that you knew the dial? Your constant use of the dial seems to have given you a vague general impression without memory of details. This is what is likely to happen when there is a lack of incentive to study. To assure the desired learning, you must study what you want to know. You cannot leave learning to chance.

Studying for an Occasional Purpose

When a test is imminent or a term paper must be prepared, study motivation is likely to be high. The need to meet the deadline set by the teacher, the importance of getting a good grade, the penalty for failure, all combine to energize study. There is a direct goal to be reached, and working toward it cannot be put off. Some students anticipate the occurrence of such deadlines and prepare to meet them well in advance. When the test time approaches they are partly prepared and need a little additional study to reach their goals. Others study only when the deadline is at hand. They study in response to outside pressure. For them every test is an emergency. When test time approaches they put aside everything else in order to study for the test. Since they are not partially prepared by previous regular study, they must start their study from the beginning. Being pressed for time and worried about possible failure they will limit their study to what they believe is necessary to pass the test. They cannot let themselves become interested in the subject because that would divert them from their immediate need. While such study may accomplish its purpose the cost in emotional tension is high.

Cramming

For those who study regularly and spread their learning over considerable time, the preparation for an examination need not require more than a relatively short period to review while keeping in mind the particular requirements of the test. Should the test include unexpected questions, the student who has mastered his work by regular study will probably be able to give adequate answers on the basis of his over-all knowledge of the subject.

If you have neglected your studies and are faced with an examination, you will probably cram. Beginning your preparation on the day before the test, you will have to put in as much time as possible in continuous study. You may study all night, keeping yourself awake by the use of stimulants. This is study under pressure and is highly motivated by the need to pass the imminent examination. The tension aroused by the strong motivation will tend to keep alertness and concentration high. The attitude of the learner will be active rather than passive. The study is streamlined, cutting out all frills and irrelevancies; it is limited to what is conceived as necessary for the test. The aim is to remember just enough and for just sufficient time to get by the examination. When the test is over most of the acquired learning will be forgotten.

Cramming is, however, a risky method of study. Should you underestimate the time required, you may fail the test. Your anxiety is likely to be high when beginning your cramming since you have no feeling of security about the outcome of the examination and your present task seems formidable. Should the test require that you show understanding rather than routine memory, you may be at a disadvantage since you have studied only disjointed facts.

Emotional tension is high during cramming. The memory for what has been studied is precarious. The loss of sleep and the use of stimulants may produce fatigue and drowsiness during the test. In some courses cramming is not likely to be effective. Mathematics and science courses do not lend themselves readily to cramming. When there is little previous familiarity it is especially difficult to learn in one session enough to enable the later correct recall of the material. When there is a great deal to learn the crammer may suffer from interference among the mass of material. As a result he may become confused. Examination questions may trigger the wrong answers.

Cramming is necessary when regular study has been neglected. It is better than no study but not as good as regular study. It perhaps gets the student by in a pinch but it is risky. Planned study is surer, bringing more thorough and lasting learning with less confusion.

Studying for Deferred Rewards

Besides working for grades it is possible to study for future rewards. Psychologists have taught chimpanzees to work for delayed rewards. First the apes learned to do work for a token which would be exchanged for food in an automatic vendor. Then they were trained to work all day, accumulate earned tokens, and put them into the food automat only at the end of the day. They worked continuously and saved their earnings for deferred rewards. The student working for long-range goals usually studies under less pressure than one who studies only as test time approaches. There are fewer emergencies. The immediate goal can be met with only a small additional effort. Meeting occasional goals becomes incorporated in the long-range plan.

Study Can Be Self-rewarding

Studying for academic grades and professional success is motivated by external rewards. Such study is done as a result of pressure from the outside to obtain goals not inherent in study or learning. Interest in the material or in the process of learning is internally aroused. Study that is so motivated is self-rewarding. The housewife is rewarded for baking a cake by the realization that it will provide dessert for dinner. She may also enjoy baking and feel especially rewarded if the cake comes out right. You may study for the fun of learning as well as for grades. It is possible to find interest in the study process and enjoyment in the learning.

In learning experiments animals are usually motivated to make the correct responses by the reward of food. This reward is external. It has also been demonstrated that monkeys will solve problem after problem, working for hours, without receiving any external reward. They find their work self-rewarding. Study for the sake of acquiring learning involves interest in the subject itself rather than a concern over its usefulness.

Some material attracts your interest from the beginning. You do not have to force yourself to study it. You seem to learn almost without effort. Some subjects are less interesting and require more work. The more interest you can create in a subject the easier your learning task is likely to be. Interest in a subject may grow. The salesman does not expect everyone to be attracted to his product at first glance. He finds that allowing reluctant purchasers to try his goods will often arouse interest in the product. When immediate interest is lacking, a subject that seems dull may become more engrossing as it is studied. You cannot become interested, however, unless you give yourself a chance. If you avoid the subject you can hardly develop an interest in it. As you persist in your study your interest may grow. It will be helped along if you look for value in it. As you find meaning your interest will increase. The more you know about a subject the more interested you are, and the more interested you are, the easier it will be to learn about it. With knowledge comes interest and with interest goes greater ease of learning.

Conflict of Purposes

Many matters lay claim to your time. Besides study, there is that letter to be written, the movie you must see, the friend you want to telephone, the club meeting to attend, athletic practice, etc. These needs may be met in orderly and systematic fashion, without interference. Lack of an orderly arrangement among your purposes may put you in conflict. When you want to study and to see a movie at the same time, you are in conflict. These two goals are not necessarily incompatible; they become so when both desires are of approximately equal strength simultaneously. Conflict arises and the student is torn in two opposing directions. If he goes to the movies he may have some twinges of guilt about neglecting his study. Should he study, he will be resentful about it, and wish he were at the movies. To be unable to make a choice will raise his emotional temperature.

Such conflicts can be avoided by providing a separate time for each activity. If you arrange definitely to go to the movies tomorrow you will not be disturbed by this desire while trying to study today. It is not necessary to abandon the goals that compete with study. Proper provision for meeting other needs will keep them from interfering with study. A schedule that allows time for all your activities will prevent such potential conflicts. Should the student's emotional life interfere too much with his study he may need help in managing his emotions.

For some students conflict centers around study itself. They are of two minds about it. They are motivated toward study and at the same time away from study. On the one hand they recognize the need to study if they are to continue in school. On the other hand they think that study is for the grind only; the regular fellow is in school for social purposes and tries to get by with as little study as possible. Studying puts you on the side of the grind. You may then get good grades but not make the right friends. On the other hand avoidance of study may make you socially acceptable but will imperil your stay at school. So you are in conflict about study.

The person who goes to school for an education is not in this dilemma; nor is the one who goes frankly for a good time. He who is not sure in his own mind about his purposes in school is in this conflict. Acceptance of study as respectable as well as necessary will reduce his emotional distress. He can then with good conscience schedule specific times for study without interfering too much with his social life.

Budgeting Your Study Time

A time schedule can provide for carrying out all your purposes in proper sequence, proportion, and balance. Adequate study times for all educational goals may be set up. Each subject will receive appropriately arranged study periods. Special study may be included for tests and reviews. Non-study objectives can also be met by appropriate scheduling.

Before setting up a time schedule keep a record for a week to see how much time you now spend in study. Look at the proportion of time you have devoted to study in relation to your other activities. Is this the way you want it? Now draw up a study plan for next week in accordance with the suggestions made below and follow it as faithfully as you can.

There is no rigid rule about the length of study periods or the number of hours to be devoted to the study of each subject. Teachers have traditionally recommended that students put in two hours of study for each class period. Your experience will show that some courses will require less time and others more, according to the needs of the subject and your difficulty in mastering it. Individual study periods need not be long. Six one-hour study periods a week will give better results than one six-hour period of study on the same subject. Psychologists have found that relatively short but frequent practice periods produce more learning than a comparable single period. Study periods may be of different lengths; some may be an hour, some less, others more. It is a good plan to schedule at least three study periods for each subject every week. In that way you will benefit most from the principle that frequent, short practice periods give better learning results than infrequent long ones. Your study periods might be arranged in relation to your class periods. An hour or a half-hour of study, including a review of the preceding lesson shortly before going to class, will prepare you for the work of that class. Your understanding of the previous assignment will make it easier to follow the next lecture and to take intelligible notes. The work of the class itself will give you direction for your next study period, and that one should therefore come as soon after the class as possible. You can then look over your class notes before they have gotten cold and transcribe them if necessary.

Short periods like the few minutes between classes or odd moments during the day are valuable for reviewing notes, thinking about your work, asking yourself questions about your assignments. A long-range schedule can embrace the entire school term so that you will anticipate midterm exams and finals.

A good schedule is one that allows for the study of each subject every day or every other day. Once you have set up a schedule that seems to fit your needs it is wise to adhere to it as closely as possible. Study periods should not depend upon your momentary disposition. Study can be effective even when you are not in the mood for it. By following your schedule, you will become habituated to regular study. Of course, you should change your complete schedule as experience dictates, but you would do well to adhere to it until you feel it should be changed altogether; then stick to the new one.

Fluctuations in the Strength of the Study Drive

Motivation fluctuates. It is apt to be high during the first part of the study period, diminish during the middle, and perhaps rise again near the end. When motivation is low, attention will lapse; you will look at your book without concentration. As a result you may find that you have not learned the middle portion of your lesson as well as the beginning and the end. Psychologists found in the earliest experiments on learning that the beginning and the end of the material studied were learned long before the middle section. An extra effort during the middle of study may help keep motivation high but some decline in motivation is perhaps unavoidable. Additional study of the middle of the lesson is usually needed to offset the loss due to declining motivation. Sometimes a brief break may revive the sagging motivation.

Under some conditions motivation declines as the goal is approached. If you set yourself to learn a certain amount or to attain a particular level of mastery you may begin with determination. When you have learned part of what you planned there seems less need to study since less remains to be done. At this point you may be tempted to break off your study, perhaps to continue another time. It may require a special effort to get yourself to go on studying until you have reached the goal you originally set. When you schedule an hour of study you may learn enough to satisfy your desires in less than an hour. Should you then quit? It is recommended that you keep to your schedule, learning your lesson more thoroughly, going on to the next assignment, or reviewing earlier material.

The Study Environment

Until you become habituated, studying by schedule may be difficult. When the time comes to study you may find it hard to begin. Evoking reminders of the values of study may get you to sit down at your desk. If you take pencil and paper and begin to make notes on your lesson you may find yourself launched in study. Creating an atmosphere conducive to study will help you. Associating study with definite cues and stimuli will in time habituate you to study in the presence of such signs.

A study desk can become a stimulus to arouse the response of studying. To accomplish this purpose it must be used only for study. If you use it for snacks and naps also, it will induce these activities as well as study. There will then be a conflict of cues. The same stimuli will tend to arouse several opposing acts. If you use the desk for study alone and do your sleeping and eating elsewhere, the desk will come to motivate study. At your desk there should be no distracting objects. If your desk and the wall you are facing are decorated with pictures and athletic emblems which arouse thoughts of recreational activities, these will tend to divert you from study. In addition to a desk dedicated to study only, a chair used for this purpose alone may come to reinforce your study drive. The sight of all the implements regularly used in study will also stimulate study activity.

The general atmosphere should be favorable for study. A room that is too hot makes for lassitude rather than activity. One that is too cold drives you out and away from study. The study environment should be comfortable but not to the point of encouraging relaxation rather than work.

Study under Distraction

Whatever tends to draw attention away from study is distraction. The noise of the radio, the sound of voices may entice the student away from study. These distractions are in conflict with the study material for the attention of the student.

A determined student can keep his attention on his study in spite of the distraction. This requires extra effort. Some students have learned to ignore the radio and remain absorbed in study apparently disregarding the distraction. Others do not succeed in giving their undivided attention to study. Some students claim that they study better when the radio is on. Evidently studying is in itself not sufficiently absorbing; they need the distraction as an aid to study. Some people seem unable to carry on a conversation except in the presence of a juke box turned on full blast. They are stimulated to talk when conditions are difficult.

Silence is disturbing to some students. It makes them uncomfortable or arouses uneasiness. They must have music in order not to feel utterly alone. When in the library they may be able to study in silence because they are in the presence of other students, but when they are by themselves they need noise in order to study. For them silence is more distracting than noise.

Background or situational distractions may be necessary to some students and may interfere little with their study. But the background may come into the focus of consciousness and will then draw attention from study. Study may be laid aside in order to listen. The talk of other students, heard indistinctly, will conflict with study. The human voice has a compelling effect on attention. Could you be missing something? Perhaps you had better listen. Should you join the group? If you continue to study you may be giving your attention to the distraction while absentmindedly turning the pages of your book without grasping what your eyes see. Undivided attention to study is better than distractability. Under distraction attention to study is maintained with difficulty.

Studying with Others

No one can do your learning for you. Whatever you learn must come from your own study. But must you study alone or can you learn by studying with others? Other people can help you. They can supply material you missed. They may offer new interpretations which help you better to understand your subject. They can listen to you recite and correct your mistakes. As you compare your learning you may gain confidence in yourself. Formulating what you know in order to help one who knows less will help you in your own learning. But you benefit most from a group if you have already learned the material quite well by yourself. Unless you already know your work you will not understand the group discussion. Your recitation will be so inadequate that you will feel discouraged about your learning.

Group study would seem most effective as a late phase in preparation for an examination. If the group is not too large and the members are well prepared, much can be gained by going over what they know together, provided that they stick to the business at hand. After general group discussion it may be advantageous to divide up into groups of two. Each one of the pair will then recite to the other. The two will take turns quizzing each other. There may still remain much to be learned in individual study after the group breaks up. Studying with others is no substitute for studying alone but it may effectively supplement it.

Fatigue May Be Diminished Motivation

Efficiency of work tends to decline as work continues. The muscles used in work become fatigued as the chemical waste products of work accumulate in the muscles. This is physical fatigue. It arises out of work and is counteracted by rest. When fatigue is felt there is increased desire to discontinue work. But the feeling of fatigue may arise even when there is little or no accumulation of chemical wastes in muscles. It may be noticed when work motivation is low. It then represents a disinclination to continue work.

When a student says he is fatigued by study, he may really mean that he is tired of studying. Studying seldom produces enough physical fatigue to reduce efficiency. In one experiment students read continuously for six hours. They were highly motivated. An electrical device recorded fatigue in their eye muscles and their reading comprehension was tested periodically. They showed only a small drop in efficiency of eye movements and comprehension during this six-hour-long study period. Being motivated in this case by a money payment they continued their work with little loss of efficiency for six hours. Physical fatigue was much less than might have been expected. It seems that even relatively long study periods produce little fatigue when motivation is high. This is not an argument against breaking up long study periods with brief rest intervals. But it does put the blame where it belongs; the feeling of fatigue from study is not physical fatigue but it is a loss of study motivation.

Level of Aspiration

How high a score do you aim to get in a test? That is your level of aspiration for that task. How long do you propose to study today? That is your level of aspiration in terms of your study time. What standard of achievement are you aiming at? Do you want to learn the poem so that you can recite it without error or will you be content when you know it "pretty well"? Do you want an A or are you aiming just to get by? The quantitative goals of achievement you set for yourself are your levels of aspiration. How realistic are they? Having set them do you persist until you reach them?

Your level of aspiration and your achievement may coincide; you may aim for an A and get it. You may plan to study for two hours and stick to your studies for the intended time. There is no difference then between the level of accomplishment you set as your goal and the amount successfully achieved. On the other hand there may be a wide discrepancy between your achievement and aspiration levels. You could aspire for an A but stop studying when you have learned enough to receive C. You intend to study for two hours but stop after one hour. There is a gap between your level of aspiration and your achievement. This is unrealistic and it may be advisable for you to bring the two closer together, either by lowering your aspiration or by raising your performance. A realistic relation is one in which the level of aspiration is slightly above achievement. In that way you may strive to bring your achievement up to your level of aspiration. If your achievement is below your ability, raising your sight by degrees may bring your performance up to the limit of ability. Thus you use your level of aspiration as a spur to greater achievement.

Some pessimistic students keep their level of aspiration below their performance. They set themselves for a C but work until they get B. They seem afraid to commit themselves in advance to a level of aspiration that is at or just above their highest potential performance, because of their fear of failure. They really strive for a higher level of achievement than they wish to acknowledge. They get pleasure from exceeding their announced modest goals. Should they fall short of their hopes they may still meet their announced goals and thus do not risk the possibility of failure. The discrepancy between their announced goals and their achievement indicates some lack of realism, but they do strive hard to reach an unacknowledged goal.

Your level of aspiration should be related to your achievement. Since achievement can be measured you might keep a record of your accomplishment in terms of the amount done in a unit of time or the degree of mastery achieved as demonstrated by grades on tests. You can know your learning achievement by testing yourself. In that way you can compare performance with aspiration and keep your aspiration level progressively a little above your achievement.

Recognition and Recall

Hearing a lecture or reading a chapter once is enough to make the subject familiar. If you go over the material a second time you will recognize it.

But it is unlikely that you will be able to reproduce an assignment after reading it once. Because it is familiar you may make the mistake of believing you can recall it when the most you can do is to recognize it. Recognition comes with partial learning but is insufficient by itself to produce recall.

Recognition is too often accepted as an indication of learning because it is accompanied by a feeling of familiarity. You may therefore cease studying when the material appears familiar and on examination find that you cannot recall it. The feeling of familiarity may be especially pronounced when the course material is clear and interesting. It is then that you may be misled by the feeling that you know the work without the need of much study. If you follow the lecture, discussion, or reading with ease, you attain quick recognition and may accept that as proof that you know the material. You may neglect to study a course for the very reason that it is interesting and seems obvious. The first course in psychology may seem so much like common sense that you may not study for an examination and then be unable to understand why your performance was so poor. You recognized the material and therefore assumed that you could reproduce it. Should you ever have to repeat a course, you may neglect to study it sufficiently because you already have an acquaintance with it; the material is familiar and therefore seems to require no study. The familiarity of the material may give you the feeling that you know it.

Observing Your Learning Progress

Mastering an assignment is usually a gradual process. You may go over the material a number of times until you feel that you know it. On the other hand you might try to reproduce your learning at the end of every trial. You would then have direct knowledge of your step-by-step progress in learning. You would not need to rely on a vague impression of successful completion of your study; you will know that you have mastered your assignment because you have reproduced it.

Observing the progress of your learning is an aid to the learning. If a learner tries to reproduce his learning after each time that he has been shown the material to be mastered, he will learn the material in fewer trials than if he merely looks at it repeatedly until he thinks he knows it. Trying to recall at frequent intervals during the course of learning is an aid to learning. Every attempt to recall strengthens the ability to recall. It demonstrates how far along you are in your learning and serves to keep your motivation high. It gives you periodic knowledge of your progress and this raises the degree of learning.

Checking your learning while it is in process may serve another function; it will enable you to correct errors. While it is not always possible to prevent error and we may even learn from our errors, no one wants to persist in his mistakes. If you attempt to recall from time to time what you are learning, and if you compare your recall with the original material, you can detect errors early and stop practicing them.

Testing Your Learning

You do not have to accept a feeling of familiarity as an indication of your success in learning; you can test yourself to see how well you have learned. If you have been testing your learning progress you will know how well you have learned, but final recall will furnish a sound basis for regarding your learning as complete. Going over the material again to see whether you seem to know it is not an adequate check, for then you may be testing recognition rather than recall. Writing out the material or reciting it aloud provides adequate testing of your knowledge. There may be a strong temptation to omit reciting some parts because you feel sure that you know them. Your self-testing, however, should be thorough. Your answers should be compared with your notes and text to see where you have omitted or distorted anything. If your self-testing shows that you are not adequately prepared you can resume study until satisfied.

How thoroughly should you learn? This depends upon the degree of importance of the subject for you. It may be that you will want only to familiarize yourself with some material, being content with partial knowledge. In other instances you will want to be able to reproduce the material or handle it with appreciative understanding. You will then use a different standard in testing yourself. The general rule is to test yourself in the way you will have to use your learning and to keep on studying until your self-test shows that you have reached the desired level of performance.

Examination Anxiety

Concern over your performance on a test provides the tension that arouses you to prepare for the test. This tension may accompany you into the examination room. It may stimulate you to do your best. If it is too strong it may become anxiety and interfere with the smooth flow of ideas. What you have learned may then escape recall. Emotional blocking prevents you from making use of your knowledge and the realization of your failure causes your anxiety to increase. Leaving the examination room may reduce the tension and release the ideas that had been inhibited. Then the answers come back with a rush, but too late, as many students have found.

Except for the occasional student who needs help with his emotions, examination anxiety can be prevented by proper preparation. When study is limited to the period preceding examinations the student's anxiety is likely to be high. Will there be enough time to prepare? Will you remember on the examination what you have learned in preparation? This kind of uncertainty with its accompanying anxiety can be prevented by regular scheduled study. Anxiety is especially likely to interfere with performance when the material has been inadequately learned. If study is carried to the point of recall rather than recognition, the likelihood of failure on the test is diminished. If you test yourself as you study, you learn more thoroughly and know that you know. All of this makes for confidence rather than uncertainty. To be really safe you might overlearn; when you are satisfied that you know your work, study it a little more so that you overlearn it. A review outline consulted shortly before a quiz will act as a refresher. Overlearning with additional review will help you to remember what you have studied. If examination fright still occurs, start answering whatever questions you can; this may liberate your recall from its emotional block. The better prepared you are the more confident you will be and the less your examination anxiety.

Individual Differences in Study: A Summary

Students differ in their ability to learn. Those who are rapid learners may get enough from a lecture or a single reading of an assignment to get by satisfactorily. In grade and in high school they may have managed well without the need to study. Some of the best students on entering college have not learned to study. Being quick learners they will improve rapidly in study skills, once they set out to acquire them. They may, however, try to get by in college as long as possible without study. Their work will be superficial; they will then be performing well below their capacity. Such a waste of talent may be avoided by increased motivation combined with the acquisition of study skills.

The student who is a relatively slow learner may increase his learning efficiency. He can use improved methods of study. He may find it desirable to devote a larger portion of his time to study. In the course of studying he will learn how to study. His learning efficiency will improve. At first it may take a great deal of study to achieve a small amount of learning, but with continued study more may be learned per study hour. Slow learners can improve their speed of learning without loss in quality. Some think that rapid learners are superficial while slow learners are thorough. Experiments on quality and rate of learning fail to support the belief that slow learners are sure learners. The evidence for quality is in favor of rapid learners, rather than slow ones. Increasing your rate of learning does not need to be accompanied by a decline in quality. On the contrary, speed of learning can be increased without sacrificing quality. The slow learner can make a deliberate effort to speed up his learning. He can check his progress and compare his present achievement with his earlier one. He can use his level of aspiration to increase the amount learned during a study hour. He can use the suggestions about improvement of study in this paper. His present rate of learning need not be regarded fatalistically. It can be improved.

Students differ in their learning goals. Some study only to reach the occasional goals set for them by their teachers. They work to pass tests and turn in papers in order to get a grade. They do not generally plan ahead but study when tests are imminent. Others have long-range goals. They study to qualify for a profession or prepare for a life career. Some plan their study so that they may reach their goals systematically; others are haphazard about their study.

Students differ in the amount of interest they find intrinsic in their study materials. Some make an effort to find interest, others do not. Students differ in their attitude toward study itself. Some embrace study while others resent the need to study and avoid it as much as possible. The latter act as if study is disgraceful and must be used only because it is impossible to get by without it. There are differences in level of aspiration among students. For some the level of aspiration is out of line with performance. Aspiration is more dreamlike than realistic for them. Others use their level of aspiration as a drive to increase their performance, keeping aspiration slightly in advance of achievement.

There are differences among students about settling down to study. Some dawdle while others plunge right in. After beginning, some keep motivated to the end of the period while others stop studying early because of a decline in their study drive. Some like to study in quiet, others prefer distraction. Some study alone, others seek company. Some stop studying when they think they know enough, others make sure by testing themselves. Some use self-testing as an aid to learning by checking their knowledge frequently as study proceeds. In all these and in many other ways students differ. With the possible exception of fundamental learning ability all these characteristics of the learner are acquired. They may be changed. A student of low motivation may become highly motivated. One who studies irregularly may study according to plan. One who has little interest may acquire interest. One who does not bother to check his learning may come to use self-testing as a means of facilitating learning as well as a way of checking progress. Students who have relied on recognition as a criterion of accomplishment may come to substitute tested recall as the measure of their learning.

How much time a student will give to study, whether he will draw up a plan and follow it, whether he will accept a standard below his capacity, whether he will be content when he thinks he knows or will prefer to make sure of his knowledge by testing, all depend upon his motivation. If he is deeply concerned about the inadequacies of his study, he may be induced to improve his study methods and to increase his study time. Other things being equal, the more time devoted to study, the more the learning.

Questions and Exercises

Test yourself with these questions. Answers to the objective-type questions will be found at the end of the pamphlet. Answers to the essay questions are to be found in the pamphlet itself.

In the following section, circle the T if the statement is true, circle the F if the statement is false.

T   F   1. What is learned for an examination is likely to be forgotten after the test.

T   F   2. The ex-GIs of World War II were able to learn more than the other students because they were older.

T   F   3. Looking at material without intent to learn is certain to produce learning.

T   F   4. Cramming is more successful with difficult than with easy subjects.

T   F   5. Interest in a subject may grow out of studying it.

T   F   6. The best study plan is one that provides for studying each subject the same amount of time each day.

T   F   7. During distraction, attention to study is difficult to maintain.

T   F   8. Group study is most helpful to those who know least about the subject.

T   F   9. Recall is likely to include the ability to recognize but recognition is not mastery enough for recall.

T   F   10. A good test of your ability to recall is to read the assignment a second time to see how well you can recognize it.

11. Which of these is not a study motive? (a) the need to pass a test; (b) the need to learn; (c) the hunger drive; (d) the need to master school subjects.

12. Using the telephone dial many times does not produce the ability to recall it accurately because: (a) there is no incentive to learn it; (b) it has not been seen often enough; (c) the dial is not arranged logically; (d) it is hard to remember.

13. Cramming is not desirable because: (a) it keeps the student from getting enough sleep; (b) motivation for study is weak; (c) the study is limited to what is necessary; (d) the learning is apt to be without understanding.

14. The conflict caused by a simultaneous desire to look at a program on television and to study may best be resolved by: (a) resolving not to look at the program; (b) scheduling separate times for viewing TV and for studying; (c) promising mother that you will not look at TV; (d) studying while the television is on.

15. Which of these is most likely to be in conflict about study: (a) the one who is not sure of his purpose in going to school; (b) the one who is in school for a good time; (c) the one who goes to school determined to prepare for a career; (d) the one who thinks that study is for the grind only?

16. Study fatigue is most likely to be: (a) muscular; (b) cerebral; (c) motivational; (d) mental.

17. A realistic level of aspiration is one in which: (a) aspiration and achievement coincide; (b) aspiration is as high as possible; (c) achievement is a little better than aspiration; (d) aspiration is slightly ahead of achievement.

18. The best way to prevent examination anxiety is to: (a) prepare thoroughly; (b) resolve not to get upset; (c) tell yourself that the test is not important; (d) keep confident.

19. Students have: (a) the same learning ability; (b) the same strength of study drive; (c) a common fondness for studying together; (d) a variety of study motives.

Try these essay questions

1. What are the advantages of studying according to plan?
2. What are the benefits of group study?
3. What is the difference between recognition and recall?
4. What is the relation of motivation to study behavior?

Exercises

1. At the end of this paper you will find a sample time schedule and a blank time schedule. Work out a study schedule and follow it for one week. Were the results satisfactory? Did you include enough study time? In the light of your experience and what you now know about planning, draw up an improved schedule.

2. The last page in this paper provides a sample form for observing the relation of your achievement to your level of aspiration. Use this form or adapt it to any subject in which you wish to improve. Suppose your spelling is poor. Keep a record of the number of misspelled words per page in your English themes and your aspirations from day to day. Naturally, you will study the correct spelling of all words in which you have made mistakes, too.

3. How many values can you find in your least interesting subject? Make the list as long as possible.

Implementing Your Study Purpose

Choosing What to Study

The need to learn furnishes the drive for study. Learning is in turn stimulated by such motives as the desire for grades, for career preparation, or for cultural attainment. In fact learning occurs out of a great variety of motives. Learning may even be self-motivated; the need to know and to grow in understanding will itself impel learning. But the need to learn is not enough. It is too diffuse. You do not learn in general; you always learn something in particular.

You learn specific things like items of information. You learn how to carry out particular skilled acts like typewriting or statistical calculations. You learn the meaning of abstract terms. You learn relations, you acquire ideas, you deepen your understanding of some aspect of the universe. In each instance you are confronted with something quite specific and definite to master. The possibilities are endless and you must therefore choose. You must decide what to study and what to ignore. You must also decide how thoroughly you will learn the different study materials.

Many of these choices are made for you. The school requires certain subjects; others you select yourself in accordance with your educational goals. Some choices you make in the light of your personal interests. Counsellors are available to help you select wisely. Teachers, parents, and friends guide you. Once you are enrolled your teacher directs you. He gives you your assignments, he tells you what parts in what books you are to read and know. He checks your learning from time to time and points out your errors. Your teacher helps to give you your set to study and to steer you to your learning goals. The outcome will depend largely upon your study skills.

Learning Is Goal-directed

A hungry rat placed in a maze for the first time will wander aimlessly until he hits upon the goal box which contains the food to appease his need. The next time he is placed in the maze his running is not haphazard. He now shows a tendency to select his route. He chooses increasingly often those paths that lead him to the goal and avoids those that are dead-end lanes. Little by little, on successive runs in the maze, he lessens his running time, and avoids deviations from the most direct route to his goal. His learning is now goal-directed. He masters the part of the maze nearest the goal box before he learns the rest of the maze. The hunger need and food incentive give the animal his direction; they determine the choice of paths. If you have no goal your study will be aimless and your efforts dissipated. When your goals are clearly defined you can see the relation of your work to your aims and choose wisely what to learn. You will then select what will help you reach your goals.

Learning Sets

A set is a direction or attitude toward your work. What you learn is dependent upon your set. Toward some material your set is one of avoidance. Other material you are set to learn. In the absence of a set to learn little will be learned. Psychologists have experimented extensively with the memorization of nonsense syllables. These consists of two consonants with a vowel between, that cannot be found in an unabridged English dictionary. Examples are puj, nof, sih. A series list of twelve of these may be shown one at a time for perhaps one second each. The list is then repeated as many times as necessary for complete memorization. Sometimes the subject is instructed to learn the list. He then adopts a learning set and proceeds to memorize the syllables as fast as he can. If his recall is tested after every presentation of the series he gets the idea he must try to learn the list as fast as possible. Even without instruction to learn he may adopt a learning set simply because he is put into a general learning atmosphere. He is confronted by a teacher and shown material. He infers that he is expected to learn. Such lists of syllables can usually be mastered in about twenty trials, if the subject attempts to learn.

In one experiment the subjects did not adopt a learning set. They merely looked passively at the nonsense syllables. After many more trials than is usually required to learn, these subjects failed to memorize the lists. When instructed to learn they had no difficulty in memorizing the nonsense syllables.

You do not need to be instructed to learn. You can direct yourself. When no set is specified you may adopt one that seems appropriate. By way of example try solving this simple arithmetical problem:

$$\frac{47}{\underline{5}}$$

What is the answer? Write it down before reading any farther. Is your answer 235? Then you multiplied. But you were not instructed to multiply. You instructed yourself, though not in words. You might just as appropriately have added or subtracted. When you are given no direction you are likely to direct yourself.

In the absence of a specific set you may adopt a general learning set. This may be exploratory, and can yield a vague comprehension of the material to be learned. To learn more thoroughly, to master the details that support a generalization, to comprehend a concept, more specific sets are needed. Reading about delinquency with a general set will give the student only a superficial idea of the problem. Following up with a search for causes will give more learning. Reading once more for evidence in support of each alleged cause will strengthen the student's understanding of the topic.

The function of a set is to sensitize the learner. It directs attention to what is relevant to the learner's need and the learner finds what he wants with comparative ease. When you want to buy a particular type of shoe you pass store windows with a selective set. As a result you are sensitized to spot the kind of shoe you are looking for. Though it is displayed in a store window among many others your eye catches it easily. You perceive it more readily than other types of shoes because your set has sensitized you. With an appropriate set you are likely to find readily what you are seeking.

To demonstrate the selective nature of set, take a pencil and cross out as rapidly as you can every "a" in the next paragraph. Do not read farther in this paragraph until you have crossed out all the "a"s in the next paragraph. Now put this paper to one side and write down all you recall—words or ideas—of the succeeding paragraph. Your set to search for "a"s precluded learning the content of the paragraph. This time try reading that paragraph with a different set. What is the effect of reading with one set at a time? Now what do you recall of the paragraph?

Generally it is more desirable to work under one set at a time. It is better to go over the assignment once with exploratory intent. Then you may examine the material with a more specific set. Ask yourself a question and study your subject for an answer. This directs you in a specific way. You may look over the material for particular information. If you are directed by several sets simultaneously you may miss important material since you will have to alternate between the several sets. Set is direction of attention, and it is difficult to attend in two ways at once, when we try we alternate directions. For that reason it is usually better to go over the same material several times, each time with a different set, rather than attempt to satisfy several sets simultaneously.

Learning from Listening

Every class meeting provides a learning opportunity. In lecture the teacher presents material you are expected to learn. Quiz sections reveal the questions the teacher is concerned about and the answers the teacher will accept. Class discussion offers a chance to deepen your understanding of the fundamental concepts of the course. You will profit from these opportunities to the extent that you approach them with a set to learn.

A passive, receiving set will gain the student little. What occurs in class will not impress such a student deeply enough to be remembered. While the teacher talks, the passive student is daydreaming. In quiz sections he is inattentive. He ignores the questions asked of other students because he does not feel involved. Listening to all questions and answers will convert the quiz section into a study hour. Class discussions are also learning periods. The student who prepares to participate and who listens to the contributions of others out of a genuine desire to learn will find himself gaining insight from the discussion.

To benefit from a learning situation you must adopt a set to learn. You are then attentive rather than passive. While the teacher lectures you listen closely, avoiding daydreams. Your purpose is to learn all you can from the class. Listening attentively is active but you can be even more active and thus learn more. You may take notes while listening in lecture, quiz section, and discussion. Not only will this result in your learning more from the class but it will furnish the raw material for further study.

Learning is sometimes instantaneous. You may hear a statement only once and know it for all time. If you listen carefully in class you will learn some of the ideas or details presented, then and there. Most learning, however, requires study. Facts and concepts must be presented repeatedly before they can be assimilated by the learner. Writing them down on paper helps to impress them. But listening and simultaneously making notes usually carry the learning only part way toward completion. The rest of the learning will have to take place in study outside the classroom. Not having learned it sufficiently in class you can continue your learning only if you carry the material with you when you leave the class. This probably cannot be done in your head, but it may be achieved with notes. Your notebook should include class discussion as well as formal lecture notes.

Taking Lecture Notes

The material you want to learn must be available for practice. Some of it is in books; some may be obtained from class and entered into your notebook. You may prefer to copy everything you want to learn, whatever its source. You can then carry your notebook with you and study its contents at every opportunity.

Your teacher says many things in class that you will want to learn. These you can record thus preserving them for later study. But note-taking is not merely a copying task. If the teacher wished to provide material for study by the student he could do it more efficiently by mimeographing what he had to say and distributing copies to his students. There would then be no reason for a class meeting. The factual material the student is expected to learn is usually available in textbooks and other study aids. In class the teacher clarifies and illuminates the material. He points out implications and applications. He shows relations, organizing material in the way he believes to be most meaningful to his students. He gives it a personal flavor.

He points out pitfalls and indicates significances. Note-taking in class should therefore include more than the data presented. It should indicate the purport of the material as shown by the teacher and as seen by the student. The notes you take should show how the teacher has organized and illustrated the subject. They should go beyond recording verbatim material for you to memorize. They should help you to understand the subject.

It is difficult to say what method of note-taking is best. Some recommend that notes be taken in outline form. Others prefer to take running notes which follow the lecture or class discussion as it occurs. Speed may be improved by a system of abbreviations for terms most commonly used. If your notes are too sketchy or too disorganized you might transcribe them in more systematic form before they grow cold. If you are not getting good results from your notes you may wish to improve your skill in note-taking. The best way would be to rework your notes every day. You could also compare your notes with those of a more successful student. In general, inadequate note-taking is likely to mean scant notes. If you write rather continuously while in class you will probably have full notes, although if you write *all* the time, you won't listen. Should your notebook become too bulky you can outline your notes, discarding what is superfluous.

What you need to learn may go into your notebook. Your choice of materials will be determined by your learning sets. As you listen to a lecture or participate in class discussion a consciousness of your purpose will help you choose the material to enter into your notebook. Your notes should include not only facts but whatever you need to help you to understand and to use the information.

Reading and Studying

Sometimes a student tries to read his assignment while relaxed in bed, only to find that he has fallen asleep. Study is active and reading for studying should occur at the study desk rather than in bed. Effective reading of an assignment requires close attention and this is difficult to maintain. When alertness diminishes, daydreams may intrude. You may then, without realizing it, continue to move your eyes along the page without seeing what you are presumably reading. Even when you read with intent to learn, your attention may lapse from time to time. In your first reading you may expect to miss some items because of unavoidable lapses of attention. A single reading therefore, will not, as a rule, be sufficient to grasp all the ideas in an assignment. It is advisable to plan to read study material more than once.

To begin with, look over the section headings and main topics by way of orienting yourself. Then you will be ready for your first reading. Your aim will be to get a general comprehension of the contents of the assignment. You are now ready for your second reading. This time you are set to make notes on your reading. Note separately any questions that arise in your mind while reading. You may then want to look over your material with the specific set of finding answers to these questions and to the questions provided by the author. When you think you know your reading assignment test yourself by writing out what you have learned.

Ask yourself what the author intended to do in this chapter. What is his thesis? Just how does he develop it? What kind of evidence or argument does he offer in support? Does he consider alternative interpretations? How does he dispose of them? Do his conclusions follow from his data? Can you detect any weakness in his presentation? Try arranging the material in the chapter in your own way, perhaps in the form of a diagram.

Outlining and Underlining

Some students find underlining an effective aid to study. It requires little time to mark up your book with a pencil as you read. It helps keep you alert and makes it easier for you to locate significant material should you need to consult the book in the future. For intensive study, however, underlining may not suffice. Outlining the chapter is then helpful. It will increase your mastery over the material. What you write down is by that very process partly learned. If you write it out in your own way, making your own outline, you do even more. You have to understand what you have read in order to arrange it systematically and your effort to organize the material in a way that is meaningful to you adds to your understanding. Making your own outline is perhaps the greatest aid in your learning of school subjects. It is creative. When intensive study is desirable, you will do better to outline what you read than to depend on underlining to aid your learning and memory.

Speed of Reading

The rate of reading differs with the kinds of material and with the purposes of the reader. Technical material will necessarily be read slowly. Novels may be read at the rate of fifty or more pages an hour. Reading for a rapid impression should be done at high speed while concern for detail will require a slower reading rate. In general, you should try to read at the highest rate of speed that your material and purpose permit, without sacrifice of comprehension.

Many students read too slowly. They continue to read just as they did when in the sixth grade. They move their lips as if pronouncing every word and carry their fingers along the line of print to lead their eyes. It is as if they were reading aloud and had to pronounce each word with care. They have not yet moved to a more skilful level in reading: reading for comprehension rather than for pronunciation. In reading for meaning tracing each word with lips and finger is undesirable as well as unnecessary. Reading seeks the author's thoughts rather than his words. The phrase rather than the word is the thought unit and the eyes can learn to take in whole phrases at a glance.

Most people read at a speed lower than their capability and most students, even the good readers, can improve their reading rate with practice. If you are a slow reader you are under a severe handicap in college. Your poor speed may make it impossible for you to read all that is required. The rapid reader not only can cover much more ground but comprehends at least as well as the slow reader. It would be to your advantage to change your manner of reading and increase your speed. You may be able to do this by yourself. Try not to move your lips as you read. Take practice exercises to improve your reading rate. Practice for as little as fifteen minutes a day may bring about considerable improvement in reading speed. There are books available with practice exercises to help you in this purpose.* Always check for comprehension at the end of the reading so that you will not sacrifice grasp for speed. It is not unusual for a slow reader to double his rate after a few weeks of practice. Should you find that you cannot improve with such self-practice, try a reading clinic. Think of the time you can save for the rest of your life by increasing your reading speed.

Comprehension and Reading

Practice with improved technique may increase your reading speed. As you learn to move your eyes rapidly across the page and make fewer pauses on each line of print, grasping larger segments of material with each eye pause, you will raise your reading speed. You will also come to read more rapidly as your verbal comprehension improves.

The more familiar a word becomes, the easier it is to identify. A new word must be examined closely and this requires time; an old acquaintance can be recognized in much less time on the basis of a few familiar cues. The better acquainted you are with the material to be read the more rapidly you will identify the words. You will also grasp the thought more quickly. In reading the eyes move across a portion of the line of print, pause, then make another sweep, pause again, etc. Reading is done during these pauses. The fewer the pauses per line, the faster the reading. With unfamiliar words many pauses are necessary. Familiar material requires fewer pauses; the eyes do not need to scrutinize such material in order to identify the words. Therefore more such words can be apprehended during a single eye pause. The eyes can move greater distances between pauses and will make fewer pauses per line.

You become better acquainted with words and phrases the more often you see them in print. Thus you learn to perceive them more easily and

---

* Among such books are Paul Witty: *How to Become a Better Reader*, Chicago, Science Research Associates, 1953; William D. Baker: *Reading Skills*, New York, Prentice-Hall, Inc., 1953; and James I. Brown: *Efficient Reading*, Boston, D. C. Heath and Co., 1952.

identify them more rapidly while reading. New terms and technical material will be hard to read at first but will be apprehended with more speed as they gain in familiarity. No doubt you have observed that a second reading goes much faster than the first reading of the same material. The increase in familiarity makes for greater ease in reading.

Studying Nonverbal Materials

Besides words, textbooks contain pictures, diagrams, tables, and graphs. Students often slight this kind of material beacuse it seems unimportant or difficult. These items will, however, repay close study.

A picture in a textbook is usually intended to clarify a point made in the text. Careful examination of the picture should therefore make the text material more meaningful to the student. The text may describe pellagra but a picture of a person suffering from the effects of vitamin deficiency will illuminate the textual account in an impressive way.

A diagram showing a cross-section of the eye illustrates the relation of the structural parts more effectively than words. But it must be studied. The student should not leave such a diagram until he can draw it himself and label all the parts correctly. Diagrams are valuable for showing relations among items discussed in the text and they therefore require intensive study.

Although the text can tell you in general about the distribution of incomes in the United States, the precise number or percentage of people in each income group is likely to appear in a table. The table furnishes the evidence; the text shows the author's handling of the evidence. By studying such a table with care you not only learn the necessary data but you can examine the author's statements to see how closely they agree with the evidence.

Graphs are pictorial representations of tabular material. They provide the same kind of information that may be found in tables but in a form that may be apprehended more quickly. General relations show up readily in graphs. They should, however, not be dismissed with a glance since close study may reveal as much detail as is found in a table.

The student is apt to consider the verbal material in his books sufficient for his needs. Being less familiar with diagrams, tables, and graphs he may ignore them. They are worthy of study because they are likely to do more than repeat what is in the text. They often provide the raw data on which the textual discussion is based.

Preparing Papers

What you need for a term paper is likely to be found in the school library. Your teacher will direct you, your textbook will probably contain some of the references you need, and the librarian will give you further aid in locating what you want. A good definition of your topic will help you decide what is relevant.

When you locate what you want for your paper put it on cards or in a notebook. You should write down the ideas and factual data that you will need. Some passages you may feel that you will want to quote and these you will copy verbatim. It will save time to put quotation marks around any material that you copy so that you will be able to differentiate verbatim from paraphrased material. A full reference including page number should accompany quotations, e.g., H. W. Fowler and F. G. Fowler: *The King's English*, London, Oxford University Press, 3rd ed., 1931, p. 15. This will make it unnecessary to consult the library a second time when you come to write your paper. For method and style of writing papers, consult appropriate manuals.*

For many students, writing a paper is essentially a copying job. Sections are lifted from several sources and strung together. A few connecting sentences perhaps, and the paper is complete. This seems safe because it is in the words of the expert authors. The student cannot possibly go wrong. While the student takes no risk he also gains no learning. Copying is a clerical rather than a student skill.

A term paper is a device for insuring learning. It is expected that you will understand what you read, will assimilate it, and prepare it systematically. It should be a creative rather than a copying job if you are to learn from writing it. It should represent your own formulation and arrangement of materials. It may be necessary to try several different plans before hitting upon the way of presentation that seems good. Because a good paper requires planning, an incubation period for ideas, and probable rewriting and revision, an early beginning is essential.

The student who is interested will find books on writing. He will also gain much from his courses in English composition. Most of these are concerned with style. The content to be included in a paper must be understood if it is to be handled effectively. A thorough grasp of your subject is essential for clarity of expression.

Preparing for Examinations

Studying for a test is not limited to the period just preceding the examination. It begins with the first class meeting. You start your study by learning in part in the classroom, and by regular study at home, long before the test begins. While this preliminary study is aimed at mastery of the subject rather than passing a test still some time off, it lays the foundation

---

* One recommended manual is Rudolf Flesch: *How to Write Better*, Chicago, Science Research Associates, 1951. For a more detailed treatment, see Rudolf Flesch and A. H. Lass: *The Way to Write*, New York, Harper & Brothers, 1949; also Robert J. Geist and Richard Summers: *Current English Composition*, New York, Rinehart and Company, 1951.

for the more direct preparation for the quiz. Without it you face the formidable task of learning all you need to know in one long study period immediately preceding the test.

Regular daily study is aimed at learning the material in segments as directed by the teacher. Direct preparation for a test is undertaken with a different mental set. The aim is to answer questions. You try to anticipate the type of question and the kind of answer required and you examine the material with this aim in view. You must learn what is needed for the test to the degree that ensures adequate recall at the time of the quiz.

You will usually know in advance what type of test you face. You are likely to know whether it will be essay, multiple choice, completion, true-false, and the like. You may also know beforehand whether you will be tested for understanding of concepts—or knowledge of factual details. You will probably have some idea of what to expect from what the teacher has said, what other students have told you, and what may be learned from earlier tests. For the sake of economy of time and effectiveness of preparation you would like to study whatever you need and nothing else during your direct preparation.

But you cannot fully know what to expect on the test and so cannot rely altogether on your anticipations. Trying to figure out direct answers to anticipated questions will probably not suffice as preparation. Some students try to study differently for different types of tests, but unless you are pretty sure of yourself you are taking a risk of missing many questions. It is probably wiser to learn the material thoroughly and in the same way, regardless of the type of examination. After you think you are prepared you may try to answer the kind of questions you anticipate on the test.

In preparing for a test look through your material and bring together all that belongs to a single topic, no matter how widely separated. Make an inclusive list of topics, perhaps one to a card or sheet of paper and itemize every item of information or idea that is relevant. Then study topic by topic. Your topical organization will give you your answers to essay questions. This will also provide you with the information necessary for short-answer questions. This method will do as preparation for any kind of test, if supplemented by self-testing with the type of question that will make up the examination. Perhaps it is better to concentrate on learning the material than to be excessively concerned over the type of examination.

Between the end of your preparation and the time of the test you may forget some of what you had learned. During the test you may search your memory, sometimes in vain, for the data that you need. You therefore need to keep your learning accessible for the test. If you construct a special outline containing cue words and phrases as aids to memory you can review this a few times shortly before taking the test and thus keep your memory alive.

Taking examinations is a skill that can be learned. This ability may improve with practice. It is not enough to take many examinations. Studying each test paper after it has been returned to try to see what was responsible for each error will help reduce the occurrence of that type of error in the future. The first test in a course also indicates more clearly to the student what the teacher expects of him and gives him a sounder basis for anticipating the contents of the next test in that course. A study of all the tests in the course is an excellent preparation for the final examination.

Easy and Difficult Material

What makes one kind of material easy to learn and another difficult? Why is the study of mathematics so hard for many students while literature is comparatively easy? The answer will be found not so much in the intrinsic difficulty of the material but rather in the preparatory training of the student. The expert mathematician, having had much practice in learning mathematics, does not find additional mathematics difficult to master. The student who has learned to read well finds the reading of literature comparatively easy. New learning, not built on a foundation of earlier acquired skills, is usually difficult learning. To the degree that older learning can be brought to bear upon the new, new learning is easier.

In English literature the student does not begin with zero learning. He already knows how to read and has some familiarity with novels and poetry from his earlier training. Most of the words he encounters are old acquaintances. It is not difficult to assimilate the new ideas with the old. New facts may have to be learned and new concepts understood. This may require some study but the reading itself gives little trouble. When such a course is considered difficult it is usually because there is so much to read, not because the reading is itself difficult.

Not all reading courses are easy. Political science may be essentially a reading course but the concepts are likely to be strange. A special vocabulary must be mastered before such reading becomes easy. The student may be unaware of this and may try to read books in this subject as he would literature. It is only as he becomes familiar with the special way of writing in political science that he picks up facility in reading. Some books on psychology also appear easy to the student. He reads along as if he had a novel before him, failing to appreciate that everyday words have a special technical meaning here. Familiarity with the technical vocabulary and basic concepts are essential for ease of reading in such books.

Courses in foreign languages are apt to be considered difficult. When you begin such a course you have little previous learning to help you. Your initial knowledge of the language stands at zero. In fact it may be below zero for your earlier learning may interfere with the new learning. Your English pronunciation gets in the way of the new speech sounds. English grammar and sentence structure may also interfere. Your initial task is therefore especially difficult and you must be prepared for hard study. Your work in a new language is not likely to become easy until you have had several courses in it. Meantime you will need many hours of practice to attain mastery. A foreign language is a new tool. You have to develop skill in its use and this requires much practice. When you have become skilled you can use the tool with greater ease in reading.

Natural science courses are also commonly considered difficult. The principal reason again is that you do not begin your study at a relatively advanced stage. You have probably had little earlier learning in chemistry, physics, or biology. You are entering a strange land. You hesitate because you do not know what to expect although you have heard forbidding tales. Since you must begin this new learning at the very beginning it will necessarily be difficult. Further, you must acquire skill in laboratory work and in writing laboratory reports. You should expect this to take time. When science becomes as familiar to you as English you will find it just as easy to work in science as you now do in reading.

Mathematics is another subject that students are likely to find difficult. While you may be skilled in arithmetic it is unlikely that you have yet developed much facility in mathematics. There again you will need to spend many hours in practice. It is in a way like the piano. You would not expect to get very far with your music without many, many hours of practice. There is a special difficulty that you may encounter in mathematics. You cannot get the next lesson until you have mastered the preceding one. If you do not practice enough you are likely to fall hopelessly behind and before the course is over you may be altogether lost.

In general, what the student finds hard is the acquisition of a totally new skill or the learning of unfamiliar kinds of material. There is no quick and easy way to pick up the new learning. In the early stages an enormous amount of practice is necessary. As your skill and familiarity grow you can learn at a faster rate.

The Rate of Learning

Perhaps you have heard that in learning to typewrite the student makes rapid progress at first and slower progress later in his learning. This is true but it does not contradict what has just been said about school subjects. The student of typing already knows how to use his fingers to hit keys before he begins his lessons in typing. He also knows how to arrange letters to form words. He does not begin at zero learning but at a relatively advanced stage. He brings to his typewriting some previously acquired skills to help him. Therefore his progress is at first rapid. Near the end of his learning his progress is slow because he is approaching the limit of his potential skill. The rate of learning is at first slow if the material to be mastered is new. Starting with zero learning progress is at first slow, picks up speed as the learning proceeds, and slows down again as the learner approaches the limit of his ability.

You may also know that the student of typing finds periods of days or even weeks when there is no apparent improvement in his speed. He seems at a standstill in spite of continued practice. Because this appears as a level portion on a curve of learning it is called a plateau. Plateaux may be temporary. After a period of practice without improvement, an increase in the learning is again likely to appear. There is no reason to expect a plateau to be permanent, though it may be. A long plateau may be disheartening or it may be simply accepted as a permanent level. Sometimes a new approach to the practice, an effort to vary it, will help get over the plateau. Perhaps a reexamination of the study method is needed. At other times continued practice is all that is necessary.

In any learning process of some length fluctuations are to be expected. There will be occasional regressions. Today's performance may be below yesterday's instead of above it. This need not trouble the learner. It is the long-range trend that is significant and as long as the learning in general shows progress there is no need to be disturbed by occasional temporary regressions.

Mastery of Study Materials: A Summary

Learning involves selection. You do not learn everything that appears in books or lectures. You evaluate the relative importance of the material in the light of your study purposes. Your sets sensitize you to noticing what you need to learn. Having found what you want to learn you enter it into your notebook so that it is accessible for study.

Much of the material you want you may find in the class lecture or discussion. If you maintain alertness and an appropriate mental set you will identify such material and enter it in your notebook. Since class material is not likely to be repeated it will be lost unless you learn it immediately or enter it into your notebook for repeated examination during study. Books may be read more than once so that that which is missed during the first reading may be picked up subsequently. Better results are likely to be obtained from approaching each reading with a different set than by reading twice in the same way. It will also be more efficient to enter into a notebook the book material that will require further study. In this way you can carry your study material with you and work at it whenever you have a little time.

You will be expected to read so much that a slow rate of reading may be a serious handicap. Slow reading does not mean superior comprehension. A gain in speed of reading may well be accompanied by improved comprehension. Increased familiarity with words and reading materials will make for a more rapid rate of reading; so will practice with the intent of increasing speed.

Writing term papers requires locating relevant material and noting it down. The material should be arranged and organized in a way that is original with the writer. A paper should be creative and not a copying task.

Preparation for tests requires some special study. Of all the material previously read and studied, which is important for the test? How can it best be used to answer examination questions? A study of previous tests may guide you in your selection of materials. Good class notes will be an invaluable aid in indicating what the teacher considers important and will be likely to cover in the test. Preparation for a test should include practice in answering the type of questions anticipated. A brief outline of cue words and phrases may serve as an effective reminder of what you need to know for the test.

You must expect to find differences in difficulty of study materials. Instead of avoiding the more difficult material you should be prepared to give more time to its study. Diagrams and tables deserve close study because they present original data from which you may draw your own conclusions. Mathematics, science, and foreign languages usually require more study than literature courses. When prior learning helps in new learning, progress is likely to be rapid though the rate may slow down as you near the limit of your ability in speed. Initial progress in totally new learning is apt to be slow. In general each practice trial brings learning closer to completion. There may, however, be temporary halts in progress or even occasional momentary setbacks in the rate of improvement. Continued practice of the material to be learned will generally result in increasing learning.

Questions and Exercises

Circle the T if the statement is true, circle the F if the statement is false.

T F 1. When the teacher does not direct your learning, you adopt a set of your own.

T F 2. Set determines the selection of materials to be learned.

T F 3. Trying to satisfy several sets at once is more efficient than working under each set separately.

T F 4. A listening set is not the same as a learning set.

T F 5. The best form of note-taking is to copy down everything that the teacher says word for word.

T F 6. The good reader is one who reads everything at a high rate of speed.

T F 7. The fast reader generally comprehends at least as well as the slow reader.

T F 8. The better you know your subject the faster you will be able to read in it.

T F 9. If you study the text carefully, you will not need to study the diagrams.

T (F) 10. When you write a paper you should copy what the authors say because they know so much more than you do.

(T) F 11. You will learn more by making your paper original than by copying from the experts.

(T) F 12. Mathematics is difficult because the student is less familiar with mathematical symbols than with words.

Exercises

1. Study an assignment. Write down what you have learned in it. Now go over the assignment to find what you neglected to learn and write down those items. What does this tell you about your set?

2. Try reading a chapter to get a general idea of what it contains. Ask yourself what is the author's main theme? Read the chapter once more to find every bit of evidence that supports the theme. Look over the chapter once more for material that may weaken the author's case.

3. What are the advantages of outlining over underlining?

4. List all the factors that make reading slower than it need be.

5. What can you do to improve your preparation for examinations.

6. What is your most difficult subject? What makes it difficult?

section four

Learning Processes and the Methods of Study

||||||||||||||||||||||||||||||||||||||||||||||||||||||||||||||||||||||||||||||||||||||||||||||||||||||||||||||||||||||||||||||||||||||||||||||||||||||||||||||||||

Introduction

Already you know something about learning and its relation to study. You understand why you should follow a study schedule, why you need to attempt to reproduce your learning at intervals during the learning, and why you need to test your learning. You appreciate the importance of taking notes and understand how to prepare for examinations. You know how to use level of aspiration to increase the amount of performance and how to raise your reading rate. These were considered in relation to motivation and to the use of mental sets in implementing study purpose.

You obtain many things by learning. You acquire habits, memorize words, symbols, poems, lists; you develop a variety of skills, see relations, and solve problems. Each is learned in a somewhat different way. In this section, the varieties of learning will be examined to demonstrate what learning method is best suited to acquiring the things you are called upon to learn. How are habits formed, skills improved, insight obtained? Three forms of the learning process—the conditioned response, trial and error, and insight—will be examined. Each of these has distinctive characteristics; each produces a different result in learning.

From an understanding of what is learned by each method and how each process operates, you may wish to adapt your learning practices to the pattern most effective for your purpose. Perhaps your present methods are not necessarily the most efficient for your needs. Whatever you can do to improve your learning even a little is important, since studying is your business. You know now that change is difficult and the first results are likely to be discouraging. The skilled way you use your present method has come about from much practice. Should you change your procedure, your first efforts will be labored, but you may be assured that you will gain skill as you practice the new method.

Conditioned-response Learning

When you want to connect a response with a stimulus which had not previously given that response, you may do so by the conditioned-response learning pattern. Thus a dog learns to salivate to the sound of a bell when it occurs regularly and frequently just before the dog is shown some meat powder. In the course of many repetitions, a strong bond between bell sound and salivation is formed so that the bell sound induces salivation when no food is offered. By conditioning, you do not learn to do new things nor do you learn how to pronounce strange words. These require a different learning method. What you learn in conditioning is to form a new connection between a stimulus and a response already in your repertory of acts. The dog is already capable of salivating to food; what he learns by conditioning is to salivate to the sound of the bell. When you want to form new stimulus-response connections, you may follow this learning pattern.

How is a conditioned response established? It may occur merely by repeated presentation of the conditioned stimulus (e.g., bell) just before the unconditioned one (e.g., food powder). This may require many repetitions. If the conditioned-response connection is rewarding, it is likely to be formed with fewer repetitions. Suppose your finger rests on a metal object which is occasionally electrified. If a light signal precedes the turning on of the current, you will not need many repetitions to learn to remove your finger when the light appears. Still another way of forming a conditioned response with fewer repetitions is to see a close relation in the new connection. It is easier to see that bell and food belong togther if the bell sounds half a second before the food than if it occurs ten seconds earlier. It has been found that the shorter the time interval between the conditioned and unconditioned stimulus, the faster the conditioned response is established. Whether or not you are aware of what is happening, conditioning will occur if the conditioned and unconditioned stimuli appear often enough together.

A conditioned response gains in strength with each repetition and by the satisfying nature of the outcome. It fades away in time and may therefore need to be practiced again. It also loses strength unless it is occasionally rewarded. If the dog hears the bell a number of times without getting food, he will cease to salivate to the bell. To reinforce the conditioned response, it is necessary for him to obtain his reward from time to time. The conditioned-response connection can be broken by interference. If the bell sound is sometimes followed by an electric shock, the dog may whimper instead of salivating to the bell.

When using this method it is important to connect the right stimulus with the desired response, otherwise an erroneous connection will be built up. If, in the experience of the child, the words "this won't hurt" are regularly followed by pain, he will learn to brace himself for the expected pain whenever he is told that it won't hurt. By conditioning he has been taught that pain follows such a statement; small wonder that a child begins to cry when he is told "this won't hurt." Make sure when you use conditioned-response learning that the stimuli and responses are joined in the way you want to learn them.

What Is Learned by Conditioning?

Habits are acquired by conditioning. The sight of your study desk may be connected with study behavior by such a process. Taking notes while your teacher talks may become habitual. The sight of a book may lead you to pick it up and read it. You learn to say "seventeen" in response to the cue "nine plus eight" by conditioning. The English equivalent of foreign words may be learned in this way. How can you do this?

Suppose you want to learn to make the response "little" to the German word *klein*. On the left of a small card write the German word and on the right its English equivalent. Look first at the word *klein* while momentarily covering "little," then look at "little." *Klein* is your conditioned stimulus and it should come just before the unconditioned stimulus (the sight of the English word) and the saying of "little" (its response). If you do this a number of times, the connection between the stimulus *klein* and the response "little" will become established. You will repeat as often as necessary. When you can say "little" to the stimulus *klein*, you have been conditioned.

Since the new connection may lose strength, you will occasionally reinforce it. Thus you can use vocabulary cards to learn the meanings of new words by the method of conditioning. You can use the same method for coupling names with dates, authors with titles, etc. Of course if you understand the derivation of a word or can see meaningful relations between the items to be coupled you will learn to connect them more easily. Conditioned-response learning occurs without such understanding, but is then slower. Although slow, it is effective.

You can learn a poem or a list in the same way. Each word may serve as a cue for the next one. One word is the conditioned stimulus which is regularly followed by the response of the next word which in turn becomes the stimulus for the third word, etc. This is the way you may learn a list of nonsense syllables, the sequential order of the letters of the alphabet, the names of the principal divisions of the animal kingdom in correct order, etc. This is laborious, requiring much drill. Poems are sometimes learned in this way. When you can understand relations between sequential parts in a poem, however, you may learn it with fewer repetitions.

Learning by Trial and Error

A hungry cat is placed in a box through which he can see some food. In order to escape from the box and get to the food, he must raise a latch which controls the door. Apparently having no understanding of the relation between latch and door, the cat tries in various ways to get out of the box. In the course of his attempts to escape, he happens to hit the latch so that the door opens.

Since the cat makes a number of erroneous responses before meeting with success, this behavior is called trial and error. The trials are not random; they are all directed at getting the cat out of the box. The attempt that turns out to be successful is rewarding and therefore tends to be repeated while the unsuccessful ones tend not to be repeated. As the cat is placed in the box time after time, he makes fewer of the unsuccessful attempts until finally all are eliminated. Meantime the successful act is regularly reinforced because it is rewarded. With repeated practice the cat gains skill in escaping, i.e., unnecessary motions drop out and the movement pattern that results in escape from the box becomes better coordinated and is carried out more rapidly.

In trial and error, the learner at first does a number of things that do not contribute to his purpose, but these are given up. He finds that one of the things he tries is successful. He retains it by repetition. As he practices, his response pattern becomes more skilled. He learns what not to do, what to do, and how to do it well.

There are two aspects to this kind of learning: the appearance of the correct behavior, and skill in its execution. The learner tries various solutions before hitting upon the correct one. Practicing it, he gains in skill. Practice does not mean repetition. Repetition strengthens an act making it less likely to be forgotten, but practice produces improvement in carrying out the act. If the cat did the same thing the second time in the puzzle box as he did on the first trial, he would strengthen the unsuccessful as well as the successful acts. There would then be no gain in skill. However, each time he is put in the box, his behavior is a little different: it becomes less and less like what it was at first, and increasingly resembles in precision and smoothness of coordination the finished product of learning. This skill comes from practice; repetition may then take over to fix it more firmly in habit.

Learning by conditioning is achieved through repetition. Trial-and-error learning occurs when behavior is varied. It is usually more desirable for the correct behavior to occur before it is stamped in by repetition. Trial and error might therefore precede conditioning. In each new learning it is well to explore and make a variety of attempts until the desired act appears. Practice will result in better performance. Conditioning or repetition could then take over for the strengthening of the newly acquired skill.

What can be learned by trial and error? Anything that you face for the first time. The baby tries a variety of speech sounds before hitting upon a combination that pleases his mother. Until he can utter the sound in approved manner he practices and obtains skill. When he does it well he repeats until the sound becomes habitual. You do the same thing in learning to make foreign speech sounds. When trying to solve a problem in trigonometry you may make several attempts before you meet with success. In writing a paper you may try organizing the material in a number of different ways. In acquiring any skill—whether it be hitting a ball, linguistic expression, or participating in a group—you practice until you achieve the desired proficiency. Whenever you are not satisfied, but try another way or attempt to improve in precision of response, you may use the trial-and-error pattern in learning.

The Use of Practice and Repetition

A distinction has been made between practice and repetition. Practice results in eliminating errors and improving the correct response. When the response is just what you want, it may be strengthened by repetition. Repetition will stamp in any response, desirable or undesirable, so the learner should practice his skill until he is satisfied before he turns to repetition.

What is the most efficient way to practice? How do you get the most memory strength from repetition? Is it more effective to practice or repeat what you want to learn as a whole or part by part? Is spaced practice more efficient than massed practice? The last of these questions has already been answered affirmatively. It is more efficient to practice several times a week than only once a week, even though the total time is the same. As long as you think of the learning as incomplete, requiring more study, you may go on improving. If you practice at relatively short but frequent intervals over a long time span the learning is kept alive. When practice is ended, learning is over. All that remains is to keep the learning at the current level by occasional use or to allow it to deteriorate. As long as you want to continue improving, keep on practicing. Not only will you learn more for each hour of spaced practice than of massed practice, but you can go on learning and improving by extending practice periods over weeks rather than by trying to attain all the learning in a day.

Should you repeat a poem or practice a skill as a whole or part by part? While the whole method seems generally superior, there are experimental results that support either procedure or a combination of the two. Because some parts may require more practice than others it may be well to go over them a few times separately. When the parts are independent they may be learned one at a time, but if they are connected it is usually more economical to study as a single unit the whole which they form. Since learning with understanding is usually easier than learning by rote, going over the material as a whole makes it more intelligible. The best procedure would seem to be to read the material from beginning to end several times to see the relations between the parts, then to practice the parts separately, giving extra attention to the more difficult sections, and finally going over the whole again as often as necessary to tie the parts together.

Learning by parts and in a single session often go together. When you try to learn a little bit of material, you are likely to repeat it as often as necessary, then perhaps turn to the study of the next bit. Learning by the whole method, on the other hand, may not be possible in a single period. It is more likely to be extended over a number of practice sessions. A combination of the whole method, supplemented by whatever additional study may be needed to master the different parts, with spacing of practice periods, will usually prove to be the most efficient procedure.

Learning with Insight

There is a third way of learning. It involves the seeing of relations, the obtaining of insight. The learner sees things in a new way or does something that he had not done before. It is not a matter of repetition as in conditioning, nor of practice as in trial and error; it is understanding. You may learn through conditioning by repetition alone, without seeing a relation between stimuli. You may improve in skill by practice without understanding the principle governing your learning. In insight, however, you see a relation between parts and wholes in learning; you see the relevance of what you do to the total learning situation.

Insight has been demonstrated in the behavior of chimpanzees. An ape in a large enclosure sees through the bars of his cage a banana that is beyond his reach. He looks around the cage for something he can use as a tool to enable him to get the food. There is nothing on the floor of the cage that can be used as a stick. He leans against a tree for a while. Suddenly he reaches overhead and breaks a branch off the tree. He now has something that will serve as an extension of his arm so that he can reach the food. He sees the tree in a new way: it contains sticks. In another example, children are taught by insight the meaning of opposites. A child is told that the opposite of "big" is "little," the opposite of "thin" is "thick." As soon as he sees the relation he can give immediately the opposite of any word in his vocabulary; he does not have to learn the opposite of each word separately by repetition. The moment he gets to understand the concept, he can apply it.

When you were a child you probably learned your prayers without understanding them. You learned them by repetition. Now that you understand the meaning of what you study, you can learn it with less repetition. Understanding, seeing relations, insight, reduce the necessity for repetition. Your course material is meaningful; find meaning in it and it will be easier to learn.

You will also be able to apply your learning to a new situation. A word like "hemianopsia" will require much repetition if it is to be learned by conditioning. If you see meaning in it you will be able to learn it easily. Look at this word. It is a long one. Can it be broken into parts? How about "hemi"? A knowledge of Greek roots will enable you to see that it means "half." Or you may recall that a hemisphere is a half-sphere. You may consult a large dictionary and find the meaning of "hemi." The rest of the word is more difficult to figure out, but you may have learned that "an" means "without." When you find that "opsia" from the Greek *opsis* is a combining form denoting a *condition of vision*, you will know this word without the need of repeating it frequently.

How may you obtain insight? There is no known way of bringing it about, but there are conditions that favor its occurrence. Most important would seem to be a questioning attitude. Where there is a problem to solve, something you wish to understand more fully, insight may appear. As long as you raise questions, seek answers, have a problem-solving attitude, you favor the arousal of understanding and insight. See the problem clearly and everything may fall into place. Sometimes your teacher can help you see something in a new way.

In one of the experiments with chimpanzees, the food was out of reach overhead. In the cage was a box. For some time the animals were unable to solve this problem. When the experimenter went over to the box, lifted it, and set it down again, the ape immediately solved his problem by moving the box under the food and climbing up on it. Thus he got the necessary insight with some help. One animal, however, could not solve this problem even with this aid. The experimenter permitted him to watch another animal so that he might learn by imitation. The chimpanzee without insight thereupon moved the box to another part of the cage but not under the food. Lacking insight, he still could not solve the problem. He learned each part, moving the box and climbing on it, but he did not relate the parts properly.

Knowledge favors insight. Facts, figures, details of information are the raw material for insight. It is the course content that must be understood and interpreted. The more you know about any subject the more insight you may obtain. When you begin the study of a new subject like physics, you will have to depend in some degree on conditioning and trial and error. As you accumulate information and skill you may gain in understanding. You cannot see relations between parts unless you know the parts. It is like thinking. You do not just think; you think about something and the more you know, the more you have to think about. As you gain in knowledge of physics you will acquire more understanding and this will make the further learning of physics easier. Information and a questioning attitude are the conditions necessary for insight.

How Learning Occurs: A Summary

Learning is change. It is the formation and strengthening of new connections, new and improved ways of doing something, a new way of perceiving a situation.

New connections are formed and strengthened by conditioning. Since these bonds weaken unless reinforced, the new connection must be occasionally rewarded. The formation and strengthening of the conditioned response will occur by repetition whether or not the learner wants it to happen. In new situations the learner may fall back on trial and error. He will then make a variety of attempts in hopes of meeting with success. When success is attained he may practice to improve his learning. Practice is more effective if distributed rather than massed. For best results it is also desirable that the initial practice be by the whole method to make it possible for the learner to see relations between parts. This may be followed by separate practice of the parts to strengthen them and finally by the whole method again to weld the parts together.

To the extent that insight and understanding occur, learning is facilitated and more easily adapted to new situations. Learning with insight increases with age, intelligence, knowledge. It develops out of a questioning attitude.

Questions

1. In conditioned-response learning:
    (a) a new response appears
    (b) a new connection between stimulus and response is established
    (c) a new insight occurs
    (d) a number of responses are tried

2. To establish a conditioned response the learner must
    (a) be rewarded
    (b) be aware of what is happening to him
    (c) be desirous of establishing it
    (d) have the conditioned stimulus appear repeatedly just before the unconditioned one

3. The conditioned response loses strength
    (a) with disuse
    (b) when not reinforced
    (c) when an interfering connection is formed
    (d) under all of these circumstances

4. Which of these is learned by conditioning?
    (a) a concept
    (b) skill at tennis
    (c) the meaning of a word
    (d) the solution of a problem

5. Which of these does not involve learning by trial and error?
    (a) learning to typewrite
    (b) being aroused to study by the sight of the desk
    (c) learning to talk
    (d) solving a problem

6. Trial-and-error learning is characterized by
    (a) practice

    (b) repetition
    (c) avoidance of error
    (d) seeing relations

7. Practice differs from repetition in that it is
    (a) more frequent
    (b) aimed at improvement
    (c) dependent on conditioning
    (d) a precise and accurate reproduction

8. While learning by wholes is generally superior to learning by parts, including separate practice of parts within whole learning is beneficial because
    (a) it makes use of spaced practice
    (b) it makes the material more meaningful
    (c) it is easier to learn by parts than by wholes
    (d) not all parts require the same amount of practice

9. Learning by insight is
    (a) acquiring a skill
    (b) dependent on repetition
    (c) seeing relations
    (d) a gradual process

10. Insight is most likely to occur to the one who
    (a) already knows a great deal
    (b) repeats his learning often
    (c) waits for inspiration
    (d) relies most on conditioning

Retaining Your Learning

Learning and Forgetting

An unusual experience or a vivid idea may occur only once and be retained for the rest of your life. What you learn with understanding and insight may never be forgotten. Some habits are so firmly established that they are never lost. Most of what has been learned, however, suffers distortion and loss of strength; it is forgotten in greater or less degree.

Forgetting begins the moment learning ends. Actually some forgetting occurs during the process of learning, but it is insignificant in amount compared to the building up of retentive strength during practice. With the end of learning, forgetting follows. The conditioned response weakens, the skill becomes rusty. The process of forgetting may be slowed by making the original bonds of great strength or, better still, by bringing understanding to the learning. What is distorted in memory can be straightened out by checking against the original material. What is lost may be regained by relearning. Relearning usually does more than revive faded impressions; it gives additional strength to the learning. What is relearned suffers less forgetting than the original learning.

Forgetting is not merely the outcome of disuse or failure to reinforce. It also comes about through interference in learning. Today's learning weakens, to some extent, the memory of yesterday's. Learning, however, tends to be kept alive as long as the learner has need for it.

Forgetting comes about through failure to use learning, lessening of the need for it, interference from other learning. Generally, forgetting is gradual but at a decelerating pace. Most forgetting occurs within a short time after learning ends. Relearning, however, requires less time than the original learning, thus proving that all is not lost by forgetting.

But how may forgetting be prevented or at least lessened? In general, the more thoroughly you learn, the more you repeat, the slower the forgetting. The more you value what you know, the more likely you are to retain it. Interference from other learning may, under certain circumstances, be reduced or overcome. An additional gain comes from efficient learning, for investigation shows that whatever makes for more effective learning will also result in better retention. Thus, what is learned by insight is retained better than what is acquired by conditioning. What is learned by distributed practice is better recalled than what is studied by massed practice. In spite of all efforts to avoid it, forgetting is nevertheless likely to occur. What is lost may be recovered by relearning.

The Nature of Memory

The memory process is apt to be misunderstood. Many believe that memory is a general ability which people possess in varying degrees. Thus some are said to have good memories, others poor ones. Many also are of the opinion that a weak memory, like a weak muscle, can be improved by exercise. Perhaps you have tried memorizing material solely for the sake of strengthening your memory. Psychologists have found that this cannot be done because there seems to be no memory-in-general. There are only specific memories. You may, by memorizing poetry, learn to memorize poetry more efficiently, but this will not help you to memorize the atomic weights of the chemical elements. Many recognize this fact when they say they have a good memory for faces but not for names or that they can remember names but not numbers. Memories are specific. This does not mean that you can do nothing about an inability to recall names or any other kind of material. You can acquire the necessary skill but it will, like any other acquisition, require practice. Practice may improve a specific kind of memory but you must not expect that exercising your memory for, say, poetry will improve your "memory-in-general." Often when a person complains of a poor memory for names, it turns out that what he should be saying is that he does not learn names easily. Much poor memory is really poor or inadequate learning. What you learn superficially or only part way you can hardly expect to remember. What you learn thoroughly is less likely to suffer forgetting.

When the trouble originates in inadequate learning the remedy is better learning. If you have difficulty remembering names, it is first necessary that you hear the name distinctly. The name will need to be impressed by repetition; you will therefore use it often, perhaps writing it down. If you are interested in the person the name symbolizes, you will find it easier to remember his name. You can improve your memory for study material in the same way: see it accurately and clearly, practice it, value it.

When you say you have a poor memory for something, you may be really saying you have no interest in it. Perhaps you cannot recall dates in history or the steps of chemical analysis. How well do you recall your school's football scores or who dated whom at the last prom? What you are interested in does seem easier to keep in memory. The effect of interest may be indirect; it impels you to study and repeat until you can recall. It may also be direct; dynamic factors like interest or need keep memory alive.

Memory is not a storage bin containing ideas intact and delivering them up as needed. What we learn is tied in with what we already know. It is recalled when the correct cue or stimulus appears. But during the process of assimilation, ideas may become altered to fit the larger pattern which absorbs them. Memories may be modified to fit our frame of reference. They may change to conform to our needs. Thus the two-pound fish we caught grows in weight with each recall. What is recalled is not a simple reproduction of what has been learned. Memory is fluid.

Another erroneous idea that is often entertained is that the slow learner has a better memory than the rapid learner. The evidence from carefully controlled experiments points in the opposite direction. When slow and fast learners are permitted to learn the same material to the same degree, the rapid learners retain more than slow ones. Of course, if the slow student overlearns, he will retain more than the rapid learner who is content with less practice. Since rapid learning is associated with good memory, you may expect better recall as you improve your learning efficiency.

Aids to Memory

Special devices are often proposed as aids to memory. In some memory-training courses the student is asked to memorize a set of symbols and use them to attach to whatever is to be recalled. One of these symbols might be a basket and if you wish to remember to bring home a dozen eggs, you are asked to visualize the eggs in the basket. Of course there is no device that will guarantee that you will see the eggs in the basket at the time you near a grocery store. Furthermore, tomorrow you may have to picture a loaf of bread in the same basket and yesterday's eggs may interfere. Using the same symbol for many memories often results in getting wrong associations from the symbol. Besides, the memory for school material is not the same as the reminder to bring home something from the store, so it is hard to see what a student would gain from such alleged aids.

There is no artificial short cut to memory. If you set out to memorize the twelve cranial nerves, you will have to do so by repetition. It is not enough to learn the names of the nerves; they must be learned in correct order with the appropriate number from I to XII. The names of the nerves and their correct order may have to be learned just as a series of nonsense syllables is mastered in the laboratory. This is a time-consuming method, and the material is easily forgotten. To save time in learning and to aid the memory, the learning of an arbitrary rhyme to which the terms can be attached is sometimes recommended. Such a jingle begins: "On old Olympus. . . ." Thus the first cranial nerve, the olfactory, is associated with "on"; the second, the optic, with "old"; the third, the oculomotor, with "Olympus," etc. A device of this kind is not really a short cut to learning and an aid to memory. You must not only learn the cranial nerves but also the jingle. It seems easier to learn without such artificial schemes which may be more hindrance than help. For example, you note that the first three nerves all begin with the letter O. The first two are sensory (for smell and vision) and the third controls eye movement (oculomotor). If you know that the forebrain evolved from an olfactory center and the cranial nerves are numbered from above downward in accordance with their origin in the brain, then it is easy to remember that the first cranial nerve is the olfactory. In this way you may proceed to use all your knowledge about the body to help you learn the cranial nerves. Artificial aids are of doubtful use, but seeing meaningful relations and patterns may help considerably.

Time and Forgetting

When nonsense syllables are learned to the point where the subject is just capable of reproducing them correctly, about half will be forgotten within twenty minutes. Forgetting continues after that, of course, but at a slower rate. The greatest amount of forgetting occurs within a short time after the original learning. Meaningful material, while forgotten less rapidly than meaningless, also suffers its greatest loss shortly after it has been learned. If material is very greatly overlearned it may not be forgotten at all. The skills we acquire are usually practiced so much after being learned that they may never be forgotten. Verbal material that is practiced a great deal may also be retained indefinitely. But it is not usually practicable for the student to overlearn his assignment so thoroughly. Relearning, as shown earlier, is more efficient than overlearning.

It might be supposed, from the fact that such a high proportion is forgotten in a short period directly after learning, that relearning should preferably occur about half an hour after the first learning. This would keep the student relearning every half-hour. There is, however, no evidence that relearning every half-hour will bring about better retention than relearning every day, or even at greater intervals.

Not all parts of the material learned are forgotten to the same degree. The first and last portions of a poem or a lesson are retained much better than the middle portion. This again is an instance where easier learning makes for better retention, for the first and last parts are learned long before the middle. It follows from this that the middle portion should not only receive extra stress in learning, but should also get special attention in relearning.

Interference and Forgetting

Some psychologists emphasize the effect of disuse on forgetting. For them the longer the period of time without use, the greater the forgetting. Every time learning is used it is strengthened and therefore better retained. This is demonstrated in a variety of experiments involving especially the conditioned-response kind of learning.

Other psychologists believe that forgetting is not a matter of use and disuse but rather the effect of interference from other learning. What we learn is forgotten, according to them, because other things learned block the recall. This inhibition can come from two directions. Earlier learning may interfere with the memory of later learning or later learning may inhibit the recall of the earlier. The former is proactive inhibition, and the latter retroactive inhibition.

There is always the possibility of interference among learned materials. What has been learned earlier may reduce the memory for what is to be learned later. If two poems are learned one after the other, the learning of the first one reduces the ability to recall the second one. This is only part of the story. Retroactive inhibition also takes place; the second poem interferes with the recall of the first. Thus there is some interference from both directions. The amount of interference among learned items is, however, not usually a serious problem for the learner. The amount of interference is greatest in the early stages of learning. The better the degree of learning, the less the amount of interference. The remedy for inhibition is more complete learning. Another fact about this interference is that it diminishes with time. This is another reason why short frequent study periods are more efficient than a long single period. In short periods there is less accumulation of inhibition and the amount that does accumulate diminishes between study periods.

Inhibition is affected by similarity. If two similar things are learned, the inhibitory effect of the second on the recall of the first is greater than if dissimilar items are studied. For this reason it is desirable to arrange your study periods so as to separate the study of similar subjects. If you are taking English, French, and psychology, inhibition will be less if you study your subjects in the order: English, psychology, French. The two languages are more alike than either language and psychology; therefore they should not be studied one right after the other.

Inhibitory effects show up in the form of confusion and error as well as failure to recall. These confusions are especially likely to occur among learned items that are similar. It is easier to make the mistake of calling "Fitzpatrick" "Fitzgerald" than to confuse either name with "Jones." Since the first part of the two names is identical, "Fitz" serves as a cue to both "gerald" and "patrick." "Smith," on the other hand, might be confused with "Jones" because they are both associated with commonness of name. Thus similarity may produce interference rather than facilitation in learning. To avoid this kind of confusion, it is important to note with care resemblances and differences when studying. Noting resemblances adds meaning to the learning but may produce trouble in memory. Observing differences will prevent confusion in recall.

Distortion in Memory

Inability to recall may be due to lack of sufficient learning strength, the passing of time since the last recall, or interference from other learning.

Confusion in recall may be the result of interference and mixing of cues. But memory suffers distortion as well as loss and confusion.

By this time it is common knowledge that the testimony of eyewitnesses is likely to be faulty. A study of the reliability of the testimony of observers will show what may happen in memory. Obvious things may fail to be noticed and therefore be altogether missing from testimony. Other features of the incident may have been observed but fail to be recalled. What is recalled is likely to be a distorted picture with perhaps some nondeliberate guessing to fill in the gaps in memory.

Distortions are especially interesting. Once, by prearrangement, a student unknown to the members of a class entered the room and interrupted the class, carrying out a few awkward maneuvers. Immediately after the incident ended, the members of the class were asked to write down what they had seen, while their memories were still fresh. Their accounts varied greatly, but one striking distortion occurred in many of the reports. The clumsy intruder was described as wearing a black tie, black shoes, and black socks. Included among those who described him in this way were students seated in the back of the room who could not possibly have seen his shoes and socks. The awkward student had actually worn brown tie, shoes, and socks. The error in this case is not too difficult to understand. In that school, freshmen were required to wear those articles of clothing in black only. It is evident that the student who interrupted the class was taken to be a freshman because of his awkward behavior. This was the frame of reference by which the student was judged and his description was brought into harmony with that framework. The result was distortion.

What is the relevance of all this for study? It shows what may happen to memory, but what shall the student do? Fortunately the student is in a better position than the eyewitness. The witness gets only one quick opportunity to observe an incident and is unprepared for it. He is taken by surprise. The student, on the other hand, knows in advance what to anticipate and has as many opportunities to observe his material as he may wish. Thus what he misses during the first observation may be picked up during the next one. He may go over his material as often as necessary to learn it well, and he may compare his memory with the original to correct distortions. In this way his recall can be adequate and reliable. If he depends on a casual impression, his recall may resemble that of the eyewitness.

Selective Forgetting

Just as learning is selective in accordance with mental set, so is forgetting. What is learned to serve a specific need is likely to be forgotten when the need is met. The waiter remembers what each customer owes until he is paid. A man who owes money may forget it but the one to whom it is owed is quite likely to remember it. You forget more after finishing a test than during a comparable period before the test. The likelihood of retaining what you have learned is better if you look upon it as a permanent acquisition than if you think of it as meeting the need of a single occasion.

Recalling general conclusions seems easier than remembering specific details. You are more likely to remember that broken homes are associated with delinquency than the percentage of delinquents whose homes are broken. It is easier to remember that all the planets of the solar system revolve around the sun than to recall the names of the planets and their distances from the sun. You are more likely to know the general conclusion of an experiment than the detailed results on which the conclusion is based.

Why are details so much harder to remember than generalizations? Principally, because details must be learned by repetition while a general principle involves understanding. Another factor may be the student's interest. Most students seem eager for general conclusions and are disinterested in details. Yet details may well be as important as the conclusion.

Pleasant material is more likely to be recalled than unpleasant. You probably remember more good experiences than bad. What you like you tend to remember and what you dislike you will probably avoid recalling. The subject that you like you will not only learn more easily than the one you dislike, but you will also remember it better. Rehearsal, attempts to recall, and relearning prevent forgetting, but this is just what you are likely to neglect to do with material you dislike. The unpleasant, being harder to remember, requires more practice than the pleasant to make it capable of recall. The student can hardly expect to confine his learning to what pleases him while rejecting the unpleasant.

Retention: A Summary

Everything you have learned undergoes change with time. The ability to recall or to use your learning tends to diminish or to suffer distortion. How can this be prevented or offset?

The first requisite for good retention is thorough learning. What is well learned is well retained. It is also true that the better the method used in learning, the better the retention. Thus, spaced learning is better retained than what is acquired through massed practice. What is learned with understanding suffers less from forgetting than what is learned by repetition alone.

Using your learning keeps it from being forgotten. Each time you use it you strengthen it. If you allow it to fall into disuse, it will deteriorate. You will stop using your learning when you lose interest in it. What you have no further need for you tend to forget.

Some forgetting is the result of interference from other learning. When the same cue is connected with two different memories, there will be interference until one gains dominance by practice. For that reason, interference tends to diminish as the new learning becomes more firmly established.

When both responses to the same cue are of equal strength, interference is a problem until one gains by repetition at the expense of the other.

Forgetting is probably never complete. Relearning seems always to require less time than the original learning. Faded memories can be revived. If you want to regain your lost knowledge or skill, you relearn it. With practice you recover your loss. It is often preferable to permit forgetting than to try to prevent it. Indeed, it is not possible to prevent forgetting. There are necessarily periods of no use between periods of practice. Relearning as needed will restore the lost memory.

Some students express fear that their memories may become overburdened. This idea is derived from the notion that the mind is a storage bin with limited content. It is not likely that you will suffer from retaining too much. Rather, what you remember will help you learn something more. The skill you retain in arithmetic helps you in accounting. The knowledge you retain from elementary psychology makes it easier to learn more advanced psychology. The things you know do not fill the mind so that it can take in more; on the contrary, they make it easier to assimilate more.

It is not wise to rely on memory when verification and relearning are possible. Parts of a story may be forgotten without your realizing it and you may give what remains as if it were a full account of the original. What is worse, you may supply the gaps in memory by guessing without differentiating what is guess from what is knowledge. Furthermore, memory may undergo distortion and in recall the distorted material is accepted along with the rest. It is well to check your recall before using it in a test. Allow enough time to straighten out distortions and to recover what has been lost. The way to restore lost memory is to relearn.

Questions

Circle the T if the statement is true, circle the F if the statement is false.

T F 1. What is learned with insight is better retained than what is acquired without understanding.

T F 2. Since forgetting can be slowed by overlearning, it is desirable for the student to overlearn all his material.

T F 3. Most forgetting occurs within a short time after the learning.

T F 4. The more you value what you know, the more likely you are to retain it.

T F 5. What is learned by massed practice is better retained than what is learned by distributed practice.

T F 6. You can strengthen your memory by appropriate exercise.

T F 7. A poor memory may be merely lack of interest in the subject.

T F 8. Memories may undergo distortion with time.

T F 9. The slow learner retains more than the rapid one.

T   F   10. Memories are stored in the mind.

T   F   11. Artificial aids to memory are not as effective as constructing your own scheme for remembering.

T   F   12. The parts of a poem that are last to be learned are the last to be forgotten.

T   F   13. An important factor in forgetting is interference from other learning.

T   F   14. The more alike two subjects are the more the learning of one will interfere with the recall of the other.

T   F   15. If you see an event and try to recall it at once, your memory will be quite complete and undistorted.

T   F   16. Everything that we learn is forgotten at the same rate.

T   F   17. Selective forgetting shows that there is a motivational factor in recall.

T   F   18. The mind can hold only a limited number of memories; for that reason we must forget some things to make room for new memories.

section six

The Value of Learning

Learning Depends on Learning

Little that you now learn is altogether new. Your ability to acquire learning in college depends upon what you learned in high school and before. Successful study in every course depends in some measure on your skill with English. Whatever you now learn makes some use of what you have learned earlier.

You bring something of your learning to every situation. You bring your knowledge of the English language into your classes. Your study of assignments, your management of examinations and skills are utilized in new situations. Having learned how to catch a baseball, you automatically catch any object tossed your way as if it were a ball. In learning to drive a car you make use of what you learned from childhood play with wheeled vehicles. You have learned to judge distance and movement of objects, you have acquired an attitude toward speed and safety, you know something about machines. Because of what you learned before you first got behind the wheel of a car, you learn to drive with a few lessons. Improved skill comes with practice and repetition makes your driving automatic. Without such previous experience, learning to drive would be much more difficult than it is.

As a rule, boys do better than girls in chemistry. Though both may enter the class without a previous course in chemistry, the earlier training of the boy gives him an advantage. Students come to every class carrying their earlier learning with them and this will make a difference in their progress. The class may be the first course in a subject, but the students are not altogether beginners. They already know in different degrees a large number of things that will help them to learn the new subject.

Skills, knowledge, and general principles learned in one subject may transfer to another. Your knowledge of high-school algebra may come into use in college mathematics. When you learn a general rule you may use it to solve a variety of specific problems. Your earlier learning can be of great value for later learning. Whether you make use of it would seem to depend on a number of circumstances.

Probably you use most what you have learned thoroughly. Well-developed habits seem to transfer automatically. You also transfer readily well-understood general principles. You are not as likely to transfer what you learn for a specific occasion. You will probably not transfer learning acquired for the sole purpose of getting by in a course. How much you transfer may depend on you. If you look for help from earlier learning you may find it in unexpected places. Looking for relations among the things you have learned may increase their transfer value.

Evidently what makes some subjects difficult is the lack of earlier learning that may be used in transfer. But transfer itself may be an obstacle. Earlier learning may interfere with later. Your ideas about energy may make it difficult to learn the physicist's concept. Having learned that there are five senses makes it harder to learn eight. This need not be a serious difficulty because the new learning may soon supersede the old, especially when the student sees that the old is impeding his acquisition of the new.

Usefulness of Learning

What is learned in school may have temporary value for getting grades. It may have more lasting usefulness. The skills acquired in speech, writing, typewriting, handling of instruments, and mathematics have potential usefulness beyond the immediate purpose for which they were mastered. They are available for use yet often seem to fall into disuse.

One reason you may not use what you have learned is that you have not learned it well enough. If you have learned to type only a little you will probably not use the typewriter. When you learn to type well, you will find you use the typewriter more than the pen. If your attainment in a foreign language is just enough to get you by in the course but not enough to enable you to read with ease, you will probably not use it when the course is over. Whatever you learn only part way, so that you are inept rather than skilful in its use, you will be unlikely to use.

A great deal of learning will be forgotten. Much that was studied may have been poorly learned in the first place so that little is retained. What, then, is the use of learning, if it is to be so soon forgotten? To this question there are a number of answers. It is hard to tell what a student will take away from a course. Some details may be permanently remembered but most will probably be forgotten. Feeling, attitudes, impressions, appreciations may remain. Points of view, ways of seeing problems may persist. Other subjects may be easier to learn because of what has been learned before. Even what has been inadequately learned leaves some trace which may make a difference to future learning. You cannot altogether foresee what learning you may need. Having once studied a subject, however inadequately, you have an advantage over the one who has not studied it at all. You can relearn it while he will have to learn it from the start.

Perhaps this will illustrate how earlier learning that has been forgotten can make a difference in thinking. In the early days of World War II it was decided to use blue filters to cover traffic lights and headlights during blackouts. This started one man to thinking about visibility of colors in low illumination. He had a vague idea from a course in elementary psychology that some colors were more visible in dim light than others but he had forgotten which ones. He then looked it up and found that blue was highly visible in poor light. He had forgotten this detail or perhaps never learned it well but he did remember that there was a difference in visibility. Thus the little he remembered helped him to question this choice of blackout color. His forgotten learning left sufficient trace to alert him to the problem.

Whatever is learned, even well learned, may not be used because the learner is unaware of its potentialities, does not take advantage of the opportunities to use it, or prefers not to use it in situations where it might be of value. Perhaps he has learned something about learning but fails to use it in his own method of study. Some people are proud of their learning and skill. They like to use it and even show it off. Having learned French they go to French movies, read French newspapers and novels, enjoy trying their French on Frenchmen, etc. These will retain and improve their skill. Having learned some history they bring it to bear on discussion of current events. Learning about art, they visit galleries. On the other hand there are those who regard their learning as something they must do in school but which could have no possible bearing on anything outside. Having learned to read they read only under compulsion. Their learning is encapsulated: it is restricted to the classroom demands of the teacher. In time they lose some of the reading or other skills because of lack of use.

The Effect of Earlier Learning on Later Learning

Whatever has been learned may have an effect on subsequent learning. The effect of earlier on later learning is called transfer. When you carry over what you have learned earlier to help you learn something new, your new learning benefits from positive transfer. If a good English vocabulary makes it easier to learn the meaning of French words, that is positive transfer. On the other hand, it is possible for previously learned material to interfere with later learning. This detrimental effect of earlier on later learning is negative transfer or also proactive inhibition. This is especially likely to be found when a new response must be substituted for the old one. If you have acquired a fixed habit of reaching for the hand brake of your car and a new car has the brake in a different position, you will find yourself occasionally reaching in the old way instead of the new. This is interference or negative transfer. Thus transfer effects may be either positive or negative. Of course, not all acquisitions have either a positive or a negative influence on later learning. Earlier learning may be altogether without effect on later; that is, the transfer effect may be zero.

New learning may occur without benefit from the old, in which case there is no transfer. If the learning is completely unrelated and has nothing in common with the old, there is no possibility of transfer. This is hardly likely to be the case except in early childhood. Most often, later learning is based on earlier and is an extension of it. Although your new learning could benefit from materials and principles learned in the past, this does not mean that transfer will take place. If you regard each subject as unrelated to every other, you will be unlikely to transfer learning from one subject to another. On the other hand, if you look for relations among things learned, you will gain from earlier learning.

Transfer refers to the use of older learning in new situations. You learn grammatical English in the classroom and if you use it outside you are transferring it. But the English taught in school will probably not transfer to outside situations if you look upon academic English as different from street English. When you attempt to transfer street English to the classroom your teacher will object, and if you try your school English outside your friends may ridicule you. In this way a barrier arises which prevents the occurrence of transfer. Since school subjects are packaged in separate units, possible transfer effects among them are minimal. Students have the feeling that their learning in each class had better be kept distinct, because the teacher might disapprove the attempt at transfer. Thus transfer may be discouraged when it could be of benefit to the learner.

Interference from Earlier Learning

New learning is sometimes made difficult by earlier training. If you have learned to say "he ain't" and try to substitute "he isn't" there will be negative transfer. The strong bond between "he" and "ain't" will interfere with the acquisition of the new one between "he" and "isn't." The new bond takes time to establish and while it is weak errors will occur from the intrusion of the former connection. Whenever you must unlearn or substitute new learning for old, negative transfer will occur.

Negative transfer need not be a deterrent even if it requires unlearning of old patterns. Its occurrence will make the new acquisition somewhat more difficult, but only during the early stages of the new learning. It is sometimes implied in the saying, "you can't teach an old dog new tricks," that learning ability diminishes with age. Negative transfer rather than age may be the real obstacle to new learning. Negative transfer is a deterrent to new learning even though it will diminish as the new learning gains strength. But the intrusion of the old learning is likely to be disturbing to the learner and he may give up the new to save himself trouble. Besides, the old pattern, while perhaps not best, is still good enough to get by on. Why, therefore, go to the trouble to unlearn the old and acquire the new? However, the learner who is willing to put up with some initial difficulty can soon succeed in replacing the old with something better.

Earlier Learning Helps in Later Acquisitions

Negative transfer, we have seen, occurs when there is direct conflict between the old and new. Persistence in the new learning reduces the interference from the old. It is different with positive transfer. The amount of
positive transfer greatly exceeds the negative. We get more help than hindrance from our earlier learning. Furthermore, positive transfer does not
decrease with new learning; it increases. The more you have learned the
easier it is to go on learning. Learning without benefit from past experience
is difficult indeed; the more you can tie new learning to your older experiences the easier the new learning. When the student does not set up bar-
riers against transfer but seeks it instead, the aid he may receive from his
earlier learning can be considerable.

Suppose you had to learn how to calculate a product-moment coefficient
of correlation in a course in statistics. Is there anything from your past that
can help you? First you may be told that the coefficient is a ratio. Where
have you learned about ratios before? What have you learned about them?
When you are told that the coefficient cannot exceed 1 does that make
sense in the light of what you have learned about ratios? You will come out
with a fraction in which the numerator must always be smaller than the
denominator. Of course you also carry into the calculation what you have
learned about arranging numbers in groups, computing averages, and the
like. The student is apt to think that the calculation of the coefficient of
correlation is something new, when in all likelihood he has learned before
nearly everything that goes into it.

General rules transfer to specific instances. If you learn how to square a
number, you can find the square of any number. Knowing the principle of
the turbine helps understand a variety of turbines. The use of principles
depends upon understanding them. What is learned by rote has limited
transfer potential, but what is understood may have widespread applica-
tion.

Transfer Effects in Learning: A Summary

Items of information may be acquired separately and kept insulated,
never being transferred to any other learning. Most things that you learn
are, however, capable of transfer. In general, the more one thing resembles
another, the more likely it is to be transferred. Where resemblances are
seen or relations appear, transfer does occur.

Once again you see the advantages of meaningfulness in learning. With
more understanding comes greater transfer. If you need to drive a nail you
may define the situation as calling for a hammer. If no hammer is available,
the problem may be redefined: any hard object that can be swung against
the nail will do. You may then use your shoe, handling it for the first time
like a hammer. This is insightful transfer.

Transfer probably is facilitated by motivation and by set. Set may sensitize the learner to find what is required to help in the new learning. The learner must want to use his learning. Wanting to use what you know and looking for what you can use will probably produce most transfer. And the more you learn the more you have available to help in other learning.

Conclusion

What you are is largely the result of learning. You learned to use language and are thus able to communicate with your fellows. You acquired a number of skills that make a difference in your daily living. Your attitudes toward individuals, groups, problems, social institutions have come from learning. The way you manage your emotions is the outcome of your learning. The information you have acquired, the ability to solve problems of various kinds, have been obtained by learning.

Learning has had a large part in making you what you are today. But there is nothing static about learning. What you are today is in some way different from what you were before and what you will become in the future. What you learn is subject to loss and distortion. It is less likely to deteriorate if it is well learned. It can be recovered by continued use, by additional practice, and by relearning.

What you learn may be kept intact. It may be related to earlier and to later learnings combining with them to form larger unities or better integrated wholes. Much of learning may be interrelated with consequent enrichment of understanding. New learning is seldom altogether new. Usually it is built on a foundation of earlier learning. The more you can find useful in your earlier learning, the easier will be your new acquisition. Learning makes more learning possible.

In a relatively new situation, the learner will do best to begin exploring. Trial and error will be the best approach. The new learning may then be improved by practice. When it is desirable to strengthen the new acquisition, repetition by the conditioned-response pattern will be effective. But in all learning, seeing relations, obtaining insight makes for more rapid progress, better retention, and availability for use in new learning.

While one method of study may be superior to another, the more you study by whatever method, the more you will learn. Following a study schedule which allows ample time for adequate study of all subjects is the best way to make sure you study enough. When you are in school, study is your job. Since there is no one to stand over you and see that you work at it, you may neglect it. You have to supervise yourself and see that you put in the scheduled time every day. Study is work, not relaxation. It requires active effort of the student. This means the taking of notes, practicing, testing the outcome, using the learning, relearning as needed. Creative use of the learning is perhaps the last stage in the process; many students fail to carry their learning that far. It involves arranging and organizing new material in significant ways, as for example, using what you have learned to write an original paper.

Learning is selective. You choose from among the available possibilities the ones you wish to master. Your choice is determined by your goals and purposes. You look for what you need in books and other sources. This gives you direction or set and the more clearly you understand what you want to learn, the more readily you will find it. Asking questions of yourself and searching for answers give your study direction. Going over your materials, first for a general grasp and then with more specific learning sets will be better than reading the material once or twice in the same way in hopes of getting all you need from it.

You learn by studying and practicing. The more you study the same thing up to a limit, the more thoroughly you learn it; and the more things you study, the more you learn. It is your motivation that keeps you studying. Your level of aspiration may keep you learning until you reach the degree of improvement in performance that satisfies your aspiration. As you attain one level, you may set your goal a little higher. What gets you to your study desk and keeps you at it is your motivation. With strong drive you will spend more time in study and try to learn more things. Your study drive is a complex of many factors. It includes your present need to pass a test. Your anticipation of future rewards and an interest in the learning itself are also included. Study and practice will produce learning. It is your motivation that keeps you studying.

Answers to Objective-type Questions

Section Two, Pages 21–22
1-T; 2-F; 3-F; 4-F; 5-T; 6-F; 7-T; 8-F; 9-T; 10-F. 11-c; 12-a; 13-d; 14-b; 15-a; 16-c; 17-d; 18-a; 19-d.

Section Three, Pages 36–37
1-T; 2-T; 3-F; 4-T; 5-F; 6-F; 7-T; 8-T; 9-F; 10-F; 11-T; 12-T.

Section Four, Pages 45–46
1-b; 2-d; 3-d; 4-c; 5-b; 6-a; 7-b; 8-d; 9-c; 10-a.

Section Five, Pages 54–55
1-T; 2-F; 3-T; 4-T; 5-F; 6-F; 7-T; 8-T; 9-F; 10-F; 11-T; 12-F; 13-T; 14-T; 15-F; 16-F; 17-T; 18-F.

SAMPLE

TIME SCHEDULE
Semester, 195—

Note: Class Meetings are printed in Capitals; study periods in small letters

	Monday	Tuesday	Wednesday	Thursday	Friday	Saturday	Sunday
7:00	Breakfast and travel					Free time	Sleep
8:00	HISTORY	Free time	HISTORY	Free time	HISTORY	Free time	Free time
9:00	ENGLISH	SOC. SCI.	ENGLISH	SOC. SCI.	ENGLISH	SOC. SCI.	
10:00	English	MATH.	English	MATH.	English	MATH.	
11:00	PHYS. ED.	Math.	PHYS. ED.	Math.	History	Soc. Sci.	Church
12:00	Lunch						
1:00	French	French	French	French	French	Games or other Recreation	Dinner
2:00	FRENCH	FRENCH	FRENCH	FRENCH	FRENCH		Recreation or Browsing in Library
3:00	Athletics	Club	Athletics	Browsing in Library	Athletics		
4:00							Library
5:00	Free time	Free time	Free time	Free time	Free time	Free time	
6:00	Dinner and travel						
7:00	French	Math.	French	Math.	French	Free time	Free time
8:00	History	French	History	Math.	Movies or other Relaxation	Date	Math.
9:00	English		English	Soc. Sci.			English
10:00	Soc. Sci.	Phys. Ed.	Relaxation	Television			History
11:00	Sleep						

There are a number of hours still unscheduled. If some subjects require more study, additional hours may be scheduled in place of free-time periods. You may prefer to schedule recreation at other times, especially to provide for viewing your favorite television programs. The time al-lotted for dating may not suit your taste. Make your own schedule or that [...]

SAMPLE

TIME SCHEDULE

_____ Semester, 195—

	Monday	Tuesday	Wednesday	Thursday	Friday	Saturday	Sunday
7:00							
8:00							
9:00							
10:00							
11:00							
12:00							
1:00							
2:00							
3:00							
4:00							
5:00							
6:00							
7:00							
8:00							
9:00							
10:00							
11:00							

Grades	Number of Composition									
	1	2	3	4	5	6	7	8	9	10
95–100										
90–94										
85–89										
80–84										
75–79										
70–74										
65–69										
60–64										
Below 60										

In the first column put a dot in red pencil opposite the grade you expect to get on your first composition. When your paper is returned, put a mark with pen in the first column opposite the space that corresponds to the grade received and put a red pencil dot in column 2 opposite the grade you expect to receive on the second composition, etc. When all compositions are returned, connect the red dots to form a curve showing your level of aspiration and connect all the ink dots to form a curve depicting your achievement. A similar plan may be used for speed of reading exercises, number of new words learned per hour of study in French, number of pages studied per hour in social science, etc.

DATE DUE

NO 16 '83			
DE 7 '88			
GAYLORD			PRINTED IN U.S.A.